SURVIVING SAMSARA

Caitlin Press Inc.
3375 Ponderosa Way
Qualicum Beach, BC V9K 2J8
www.caitlin-press.com

Cover and text design by Vici Johnstone
Edited by Holly Vestad
Cover photo by Sirisvisual via Unsplash
Printed in Canada

Caitlin Press Inc. acknowledges financial support from the Government of Canada and the Canada Council for the Arts, and the Province of British Columbia through the British Columbia Arts Council and the Book Publisher's Tax Credit.

Library and Archives Canada Cataloguing in Publication

Title: Surviving samsara : a memoir of breakdowns, breakthroughs, and mental illness / Kagan Goh.

Other titles: Surviving samsara (2021)
Names: Goh, Kagan, 1969–, author.

Identifiers: Canadiana 20210274735 | ISBN 9781773860329 (softcover)
Subjects: LCSH: Goh, Kagan, 1969-—Mental health. | LCSH: Manic-depressive persons—Canada—Biography. | LCSH: Manic-depressive illness—Religious aspects. | CSH: Authors, Canadian (English)—21st century—Biography. | LCGFT: Autobiographies.

Classification: LCC RC516 .G64 2021 | DDC 616.89/50092—dc23

Surviving Samsara

A Memoir of Breakdowns, Breakthroughs, and Mental Illness

KAGAN GOH

CAITLIN PRESS 2021

This book is dedicated to my beloved wife,
soulmate, and love of my life,
Julia Hogeling-Goh,
without whom I would not know
the meaning of unconditional love.

This book is also dedicated to my mother and father,
Margaret Joyce Wong and Goh Poh Seng,
whose guiding light
leads me through the dark forest of the night.

And to my fellow mental health veterans,
who constantly inspire me
with their courage, resilience, and fortitude,
teaching me time and again
that at the darkest hour comes the light.

Surviving Samsara is a true story. Some of the names have been changed to protect people's identities; others remain unchanged.

It is about the trauma of mental illness. It deals with mania, psychosis, hallucinations, shame, guilt, hypersexuality, depression, attempted suicide, suicidal ideation, and the devastating aftermath of a diagnosis. This is difficult subject matter. It is also my lived experience.

But this memoir is also about my transformation. I came of age through mental illness. I grew because of, not despite, this difficult subject matter.

Samsara: "'Round of rebirth,' lit. 'perpetual wandering,' is a name by which is designated the sea of life ever restlessly heaving up and down, the symbol of this continuous process of ever again and again being born, growing old, suffering and dying. More precisely put, samsara is the unbroken chain of the fivefold khandha-combinations, which, constantly changing from moment to moment, follow continuously one upon the other through inconceivable periods of time. Of this samsara, a single lifetime constitutes only a tiny and fleeting fraction; hence to be able to comprehend the first noble truth of universal suffering, one must let one's gaze rest upon the samsara, upon this frightful chain of rebirths, and not merely upon one single lifetime, which, of course, may be sometimes less painful."

—Buddhist Dictionary by Nyanatiloka Mahathera

Contents

INTRODUCTION

When people ask, "Who are you?" I answer, "My name is Kagan Goh."

Invariably, the next question is, "What do you do?"

"I am an MD."

"A medical doctor?"

"A manic depressive. Certified."

When my MD—that is, my real medical doctor—told me I had an incurable illness that would last my whole life, I decided then and there that I would embrace it as my full-time job, a professional manic depressive, educating people about issues affecting those of us with mental illness. So, here I am, your own personal, professional, manic depressive, at your service. What would you like to know? What is Samsara? Have you heard of Nirvana? Well, Samsara is the opposite of Nirvana. According to the Buddhist Dictionary: "Samsara is defined as the 'round of rebirth' or 'perpetual wandering' ... the sea of life ever restlessly heaving up and down, the symbol of this continuous process of ever again and again being born, growing old, suffering and dying." It is the kind of tumult that occurs in everyday life, from movement from the uncontrollable shift from high to low, from joy to despair, from exultation to depression, from reality to illusion to delusion and back again. I use Samsara as a metaphor to describe the out of control roller coaster ride through the highs of mania, the terrors of psychosis, and the lows of depression of my lived experience with manic depression.

People are both fascinated and scared of manic depression because it is a mental illness that affects one's moods and emotions. Perhaps they are afraid that they too have the potential to become 'crazy.' A traumatic event—such as losing one's job, the death of a loved one, being evicted from one's home, or a divorce—can trigger a mental health breakdown. Many of us are one paycheque away from living on the streets. Take two steps backward and fall into the abyss. The reality is that we are all standing on the edge of the precipice.

I was diagnosed as manic depressive in 1993 on Valentine's Day of all days. I prefer the term manic depression to the clinical and politically correct term bipolar because it more accurately describes my own personal lived experience of both the highs of mania and the lows of depression that characterize this condition. The reader might find it incredulous and unbelievable that this story is true, since many of its events and situations seem fictional; dare I say outlandish, fantastical, and even surreal. But as the saying goes: truth is stranger than fiction. Some readers may presume I am employing a literary device, taking artistic licence by using magic realism in my storytelling. Diagnosed with a bipolar condition (a.k.a. manic depression), I have been prompted by the extraordinary hallucinations, visions, and manic psychotic and depressive episodes I have experienced to coin a new term: manic realism.

I hope to give the reader insightful, compassionate, and validating depictions of altered psychological states in this book. I hope this book gives the reader intimate insights into an "insider's" experience of madness. It's not just showing psychosis as an illness but also as a valid and valuable form of neurodiversity that is a part of a healing process that the psyche is undergoing. I hope this book becomes a lifesaver for people with mental illness, providing a roadmap of how to navigate the mental health system and avoid the pitfalls I encountered. I wish the book will become an influential eye-opener for people working in mental health fields. I envision literature being used as a tool for community outreach. My story provides a rare opportunity to see (and empathize with) what mental illness and recovery look like from the inside. May this book expand the conversation around mental health.

SURVIVING SAMSARA

December 26, 2000

My mind is consumed by raging fire. I scream in excruciating pain. Leaning over the edge of the Burrard Street Bridge, I am tempted to jump into False Creek to extinguish the flames. I climb up onto the railing. I balance atop it, looking down. The water sparkles like a diamond tiara as I spin the roulette wheel of Samsara. I must extinguish my anguish. I turn back to see the world one last time. The bright sunny morning mocks me. It is annoyingly cheerful. The traffic flies past me, oblivious to my plight. I am one insignificant man, in an overpopulated planet of seven billion suffering souls, desiring death.

My head spins as I picture myself plummeting into the icy water. Into oblivion. I walk the tightrope in my head. One false step and I'm dead.

JOY

July 1, 1990

I am at a house party in Ottawa when I meet a woman named Joy.

"It's a joy to meet you, Joy," I say.

She beams at me, then says, "I am manic-depressive."

The conversation ends before it really began. Not knowing what to say, I make an excuse: "I have to call my girlfriend."

A lie. I avoid her all night, staying upstairs while she waits below, lost in the party.

She reminds me of a dog I once had when I was eight years old. He was always happy to see me, jumping up and licking my face. Overwhelmed by his affection, I fled upstairs, afraid to come down.

Eventually my mother lost her patience. "Okay, we'll give him away to the SPCA."

She made me accompany her. I carried the dog in my arms. He looked at me and I saw tears in his eyes.

He spoke to me: *Don't leave me.*

When we arrived at the SPCA, I said, "Mum, I've changed my mind. I want to keep him."

"No," she replied. "After all the trouble you've caused me, dragging me all the way here, you don't deserve a dog."

This is how I would come to feel every time I was led back to the psych ward: an obedient dog crying to God, *Don't leave me.*

Spies in the House of Love

February 14, 1993

As night encroaches, the temperature drops and a chill enters my weary bones. I am hungry and looking for some grub. Some panhandlers tell me that free food will be served after service at the church down the street. I decide to get out of the rain and head there.

The First Baptist Church on Nelson and Burrard is a grey stone-slabbed fortress. Its cathedral towers into the sky, asserting the church's power. As I approach it, I am intimidated by its authority. It resembles a castle more than a church. All that is missing is a drawbridge and a moat. I choose to go with the flow of the crowd, entering the gaping mouth of the church like Jonah swallowed into the belly of the whale.

Inside the church, I take my seat. A black man seated in the bench in front of me turns around, nods his head, and grins wickedly at me, his white teeth gleaming as if he were in a toothpaste commercial. I look down at my street clothes: I am wearing a green hippie tie-dye T-shirt, Thai batik quilted patchwork pants, and torn black cut-off jeans. I do not fit in with this respectable upper-middle-class congregation. I have come in from the cold to warm myself in God's home and hopefully get a free meal, and I get the sense that everyone can tell. Just before the sermon begins, the church altar boy hands out the money basket. I watch as the crowd drops in coins, bills, things I don't have.

When it is handed to me, I look inside my backpack to see what I can share. I see the stale but still edible day-old bread that I found in a dumpster outside a bakery and drop it into the basket. I am proud of the symbolic offer: to me, the loaf of bread symbolizes the body of Christ. I pass the basket to the woman sitting beside me. She looks repelled by my offering and quickly hands the basket to the next person beside her.

I catch the church altar boy raising his eyebrow and looking at me suspiciously. He leans over to the priest and whispers something into her ear. I can read their minds: "Keep your eye on this joker. He stinks of trouble."

I am enjoying the priest's sermon about Christian charity. She lectures to the congregation that they have a moral obligation as good Christians to watch out for the poor and disenfranchised. She inspires me to speak when she preaches of being "our brother's keeper." She makes an announcement during her sermon: "If anyone has something to say, you are welcome to make an announcement after the sermon. Since today is Valentine's Day, we will be serving food and refreshments after the service."

I certainly have something to say. First and foremost, I want to tell the congregation about the street kids who have been evicted from their rooming house, called Street Kids in Distress. The people with clout want to kick them out. Truth be told, it is just an excuse for the rich land developers to appropriate the prime downtown property to develop condominiums. Therefore, they evict the kids for some bogus housing bylaw. I am going to tell the congregation to take whatever leftover food there is from the banquet and to share it with the street kids. More importantly, I am going to encourage the congregation to talk directly to the street kids and find out what is going on in their lives. The good citizens can then champion their cause by talking to their local legislators. They have more clout as respectable taxpaying citizens. Perhaps if they speak on behalf of the street kids, the politicians in city council would listen to these kids' plight. Listen to the cries of these kids. These kids are our future, these children are our children, and we must look out for them. It is my belief that Valentine's Day should not be just about romantic love; it should also encompass love for our common humanity.

I feel inclined to speak up. I rise from my bench and excuse myself as I shuffle my way down the aisle toward the front of the altar. I am in a deep trance as I walk past my fellow worshippers. I stand under the stage, staring up at the podium where the preacher is delivering her sermon. Two altar boys, dressed in ceremonial black garb, swiftly approach me. "Would you please sit down?" they sternly whisper.

I nod, obey, take my seat in the front row. I pay attention once more to the sermon. The preacher is using the metaphor of Christ as a fisherman who catches rainbow-coloured fish one after the other with a fishing line attached to a hook with no bait. I am immediately reminded of my recurring dream about fishing in the ocean with an empty hook, where I catch multiple rainbow-coloured fish.

I don't want to be the Fisher King.

I'd rather be the Fisher Prince.

The preacher quotes a passage from the Bible: "'And I will make you fishers of men.'"

Just like a line of poetry I wrote earlier today:

> Shed the snakeskin of your skepticism
> I shall make you fishers of men
> That is who I am:
> The Fisher Prince

Upon hearing the preacher's words, I am struck by a thunderbolt from God. I stand back up with my arms outstretched in exultation.

"Please come with me," commands a stern altar boy.

There is going to be trouble, a voice in my head warns me. *But do as they say. Do not resist.*

I behave politely, following the two altar boys down the aisle away from the service and the rest of the worshippers, who look at me, perplexed.

The two altar boys lead me down a flight of stairs into a dark basement. I follow them. One turns to me and says, "Tell us what you want to say to the congregation."

They are interrogating me. They are trying to intimidate me. I feel their dark, menacing presence. I refuse to answer their questions.

"That is for me to share with everybody, not with you."

I know who they really are. They are agents of the Devil, imposters pretending to serve God. They are spies in the House of Love.

I am beginning to feel paranoid.

I turn to a child's drawing of Noah's ark hanging on the wall. I begin to explain the significance of the symbolism of the picture. The altar boy interrupts me as I am speaking.

"That's just a drawing made by little children. It means nothing."

"Children can see things you will never understand."

The two have me cornered. I decide to break the stalemate. "Get out of my way!"

I wave my hand and envision throwing them aside with the invisible force of my chi energy. I walk past them down the corridor. Frightened, I hear the roar of the Devil at my heels, screeching like a train wreck. Everything happens in slow motion. The darkness is rushing from behind me with a swoop.

As I walk up the stairs, I feel as if I were walking underwater. Demons grasp at my ankles. Any sound I hear is distorted like a tape recorder set to rewind. In this moment I am confident that I can walk through fires unscathed.

As I climb the steps, I repeat a mantra: "I AM THE LORD AND THE LORD IS ME. I AM THE LORD AND THE LORD IS ME. I AM THE LORD AND THE LORD IS ME."

I pray: "God be with me now in my darkest hour."

I arrive at the main floor and walk into the light. I head for the podium. I must tell the worshippers.

Before I have a chance to react, the weight of the Devil collapses me to the floor. I land hard on the stone floor, struggling under his weight. I catch a glimpse of a badge, guns. My skin chafes against a thick, starched synthetic. Cops. One. Two. Five. Eight. They wrestle me to the ground and spray mace in my eyes. They are agents of the Devil, demons attempting to claim my soul.

Expensive heels scuff the stone floor. Women scream and children holler. The congregation rises in an uproar of shock and confusion. I shout as the cops drag me out into the foyer. A forearm wraps itself around my neck and tenses. Silencing me. I am suffocating.

I squirm and cry for help: "I can't breathe!"

A voice in my head cries out, *Don't resist!*

I let my body go limp as a puppet. The forearm releases. My eyes are burning; tears stream down my cheeks.

I sense one positive presence. A cop kneels beside me and begins pouring gel over my eyes to stop the burning.

"Here you go."

He is gentle.

"This will help stop the burning."

I trust him.

"You will feel better soon."

"You're very kind. Thank you very much."

They lift me up from the floor and guide me outside the building. In the back alley, I am slammed against a wall and handcuffed by an officer.

With a smirk in his voice he says, "This hurt?"

Still reeling from my visions, I reply, "Nah, this is only physical pain. Nothing compared to the spiritual pain you're going to go through."

He throws me into the back seat of the police car. The lights flare. He drives me to the police station on Hastings and Main.

While I am being fingerprinted, I use the black ink from the ink pad and start to draw a picture with my ink-stained fingers for the arresting officer, saying, "This is for you. Keep it. I am going to be a famous artist someday. It will be worth a lot."

"Yeah buddy, I'm sure it's worth a fortune."

As I exit the room, I watch as he crumples up the drawing and throws it into the waste bin, nodding to his colleague. "In this line of work, sooner or later you meet all sorts of kooks."

They throw me into solitary confinement in a cell that is slightly bigger than a coffin. I am in complete darkness. My clothes are torn. I feel scratches all over my body. The two possessions the cops do not take away are my necklace and a tube of shower gel I found earlier on the street.

In the darkness, I enter a psychic state of mind. I take off all my clothes and smear the gel all over my body as a form of protection.

I am in a trance.

The cell door opens. I squint at the silhouette of a police officer. "What's your name?"

I refuse to answer.

"You're not getting out of here until you tell us your name." The door closes and I hear the latch.

I am furious. Without delay, I am in the mind of God. I have the power to induce an earthquake to shatter the building. I am so angry that I have the power of God to break free from the cell, climb out of the rubble to freedom.

But my godlike powers do not materialize.

I am trapped in a cell on the darkest side of hell.

Time passes. Having no watch, I lose track of how long I've been in the cell. I feel like I've been trapped in this hellhole for an eternity.

Eventually, the cops order that I dress myself and I am moved to another cell with eight other inmates.

I walk to the sink in the corner, strip off my clothes, and start to wash the gel off my body. Soap bubbles seem to appear out of nowhere. My body is covered in soapsuds. I ignore the stares from the inmates, wash myself clean, and towel off.

The inmates go to bed. I am in a state of superconsciousness. I weave the happy dreams of my cellmates' childhoods together. I hear my cellmates start to talk in their sleep, babbling like happy kids. I bear witness to these hardened criminals talking like little children. I am the Dreamweaver. I think, *Even criminals are innocent when they dream.* I don't sleep.

The next morning, the cop strikes a bargain with me. "Tell us your name and we'll grant you one phone call."

I am exhausted, but the paranoia has momentarily passed. "My name is Kagan Goh."

I am led to a phone. I call home. Mum answers the phone.

"Kagan, you didn't come home last night." Her voice is strained.

"I am worried sick. Where are you?"

"I am in jail." I break out in laughter, finding the situation absurd. Mum is not amused.

✑

The police report describes me as a "drunk Native." My request to have a Breathalyzer test falls on deaf ears. I am also charged with causing a disturbance in the church by yelling and fighting with the police officers. I protest the statement. But who would believe the words of a Chinese-Canadian youth with tanned skin and torn clothing, heavy with connotation? It is the words of eight cops against mine.

"Your discriminatory treatment of me is indicative of the systemic racism against Indigenous people in Canada!" I shout at the officers. Judging by the looks on their faces, my words only confirm my status as a "kook."

✑

Dad posts my bail and picks me up from the police station.

"You are not well, Kagan," says Dad.

He clutches my arm; although Parkinson's has made his body frail, his grip today is tight and firm. He leads me back to the car, shutting and locking the door. We sit together silently. He starts the engine and drives me home.

✑

My behaviour concerns my parents. They invite Uncle Chin Chee Nan, a psychiatrist, to visit me at home. One afternoon, I find myself sitting across from him in my parents' living room.

"Kagan, your parents are concerned about you," says Uncle Chee Nan. "They say you have been behaving strangely."

I am being tested. I must answer his questions with complete honesty. My body trembles in fear. I tell my uncle about my friendship with the street kids. I tell him about my spiritual visions and revelations in the church. I recount my altercation with the police.

"Spiritual delusions. God ideation." Uncle Chee Nan exchanges a quick glance with my parents. "In my opinion, I strongly suspect Kagan suffers from manic depression, also known as bipolar disorder."

"What is manic depression?"

"Manic depression is a mental illness, characterized by extreme highs and extreme lows." Uncle Chee Nan gives us a moment to process. "I have good news and bad news."

"What's the bad news?" I ask, wanting to get it over and done with.

"You have an incurable illness that will last your entire life."

The words cast a claustrophobic net over the living room. "And the good news?" I can barely make the sound.

"The charges against you for causing a disturbance in a church and fighting with the police officers will likely be dropped because of the diagnosis."

My uncle gets up to leave. "I will go now on the condition that I can come back any time to visit you."

I agree and shake his hand. It is cold to the touch, sending shivers up my spine. I see my uncle out the door, knowing that someday he will return to visit not his nephew but his patient.

WE BELONG TO THE WIND

March 1996

My day now nearly spent, I have an urgent need to return home to Daniela, the Love that I love who waits, always, as I complete my day's daydreaming. I take the scenic route, preferring to walk the back alley to our house at the top of the hill rather than the pavement of the main streets, fronted by quaint character houses with manicured lawns and perfected gardens. Along the way, I pick wildflowers growing up through the dirt between fence slats. I follow the path of hundreds of black crows migrating to their sanctuary for the night. My haven is with Daniela in the cozy basement apartment of my parents' house. We are blessed to have a wild Garden of Eden in the backyard. Our allotted acre of paradise. We are young and we are in love.

I carry my hand-picked bouquet of wildflowers and sing out loud, not caring who hears this mad fool's love song.

> Up there lies ahead
> The Love that I love
> The Love that I love
> Up there lies ahead
> The Love that I love
> The Love that I love

> You, my dear, whom I adore
> walking uphill to our door
> Be my love forevermore
> in this ever-changing world
> where nothing's sure

No matter how hard my day went
coming home to you I'm heaven sent
Work so hard to make a cent
in your arms I feel innocent

You open the door to let me in
greeting me with a happy grin
I'm the luckiest man in the whole wide world
staying at home with my loving girl

I wonder why I have been blessed
with this earthbound simple happiness
What have I done to deserve such love?
Does God smile upon me from above?

Under the roof of our happy home
living with you I'm not alone
for you are the one that I adore
every time I walk home to our door

Up there lies ahead
The Love that I love
The Love that I love
Up there lies ahead
The Love that I love
The Love that I love

I enter the back gate and knock on the door.

Daniela answers. I hold up my bouquet.

"Thank you for the lovely flowers." She flings her arms around me. "I was listening to you sing as you walked up the alley. That's the most beautiful song I've ever heard."

We kiss unabashedly. Drunk on desire, we retreat indoors for the night.

❧

The next morning, I watch Daniela while she sleeps. All is quiet except for the faint whisper of breath. Daniela rests her head upon my chest. I watch her sleep and wish I were a sunbeam that would wake her gently each morning. Our black cat, Tarim, crawls into bed and curls at our feet, warm and familiar. I run my hands through Daniela's blond hair and lean over to kiss her lips. A smile spreads lazily across her face.

"Tell me about the first time you saw me," she says.

"You've heard it a million times."

"Tell me again."

I prop my head up on my hand and give her a lazy smile back. "I took some time off of university to backpack through Southeast Asia and Europe. I met you at a nightclub in Berlin called the Bunker. Here I was—a disoriented Asian boy from Singapore—and you—an eastern European chick from Germany—meeting at the crossroads of East and West. Amid the deafening techno music and flashing strobe lights, I noticed you staring at me from across the smoky dance floor. My first thought was 'This is the most beautiful woman I have ever laid my eyes on.' And my second thought was 'I'll never be with you.'"

"I am shy by nature, but for once I didn't avert my gaze, and I stared back at you," says Daniela.

"Our eyes locked from opposite sides of the room as we slowly walked a beeline toward each other. The throng of sweaty dancers' colliding bodies parted for us the way the Red Sea must have parted for Moses. Without saying a word, we met in the middle. Facing each other, you flashed me the most seductive smile, dripping with lust."

"We started to kiss, making out right there on the dance floor," Daniela recalls. "That was a night that I'll never forget."

"I thought I would never see you again. I didn't even know your name, but I guess I told you mine. I was so surprised when I received your letter."

Daniela beams up at me. "And it's been three happy years."

"Never in my wildest dreams did I imagine you would end up living with me. Miraculously, today you are in my arms. It's fate."

I look into her bright blue eyes. "You and I took the leap, and here we are."

Afterwards, Daniela traipses naked to the bathroom, turns on the water. I follow. She steps into the scalding hot shower and rinses. I join her. I am on my knees soaping her body when she pinches the flesh on her belly and laments, "Look how fat and ugly I've become. I've got gross cellulite on my thighs."

"You are beautiful. You are perfect just the way you are. I love you now. I will love you when you are old and grey."

"Be honest with me. I'm growing old."

"I don't know what you are talking about," I reply.

But that isn't the answer she wants. In the shower we become grotesque. As she shaves her legs, I see a vision of us in the future when we're grey haired, varicose veined, flesh shrivelled: a phantasmagoria of anatomical horrors.

"I feel old and ugly. I want to be young again," complains Daniela.

I smile. Oh, the narcissistic vanity of youth.

❧

Daniela performs a home pregnancy test in the bathroom. We wait anxiously. The test stick doesn't change colour. Daniela's not pregnant.

I breathe a sigh of relief. Daniela is sad and disappointed. I hold her, cradling her in my arms, but she becomes inconsolable. She feels that we failed God's litmus test to see whether we were ready to take our relationship to the next level. She pries herself out of my arms and spends the rest of the day curled up in bed under the cloak of our duvet.

I sit next to her on the bed and put my hand on her shoulder. "It wasn't the right time, Daniela."

She tosses around and turns her back to me. "I want to have your baby." Her voice is muffled from underneath the covers.

"We're only in our twenties. We're still young. There's still plenty of time to have kids." She turns to face me and I take her in my arms. "I have so many dreams I want to fulfill with you," I confide. "I want to travel the world with you."

Some days I am in such bliss that I want to propose to Daniela, but I have always held back, waiting for the perfect moment. I wanted to do it in a grandiose way. I envisioned us climbing to the summit of a Himalayan mountain, where I ask her to marry me on the top of the world.

"We've been together for three years. If you're not ready now, when will you ever be ready?" she laments.

She's right. What am I waiting for?

The next day I visit a jewellery shop in Chinatown.

☙

Two weeks later and the flowers are blooming in our Garden of Eden. I choose this perfect beautiful spring morning to spring a surprise on Daniela.

"I've got a present for you." She sits up from the unmade bed. I hand her a tiny box. "I had this custom-made."

Daniela opens it and gasps. Inside is a gold ring embossed with a Chinese character.

"The symbol of Double Happiness," I say. "These Chinese characters symbolize two joyful soulmates holding hands in sacred union. Each partner stands like a pillar supporting the roof of a house. They remain individuals, but their joined hands unite them, forming a strong foundation of the relationship. In this way, the couple maintains their independence while supporting each other in their marriage, thus doubling their happiness as husband and wife."

I get down on one knee. "Will you marry me?"

Daniela's blue eyes dance like the ocean. She touches her gold crucifix around her neck as if her prayers have been answered.

"I've been waiting forever for you to ask," she says, tearing up. "Yes, I will marry you."

I stand up and slip the ring on her finger. She kisses and hugs me.

"Nothing can come between us." I kiss her on the forehead, blessing her like a priest. "After we are married, not even God can tear us apart. I love you more than anyone else. More than the Father, Son, and Holy Ghost." I am caught up in romantic rapture. The words escape from me—and surprise me as I say them.

Daniela is put off by my faux pas. We are both frozen for a moment.

"This is a bad omen," she says, backing away from me. The look of adoration on her face melts into one of superstition. "I just had a dreadful premonition. You are a blasphemer tempting fate because you love me more than God."

"Daniela. Stop this nonsense!" I grab her shoulders, surprised by her conviction.

"I predict that a jealous God, a force greater than us, will drive us apart."

I try to grasp her hands. She recoils from my touch. "It pains me to know that there are roads within you I will never travel," she says.

"What do you mean?"

She pries herself away from me. "I would love to be your sole companion, but there are roads you must travel alone—without me."

Daniela begins to pray like a cloistered nun, her fingers interwoven so tight that her knuckles turn white.

"You're going to go on without me," she says to me.

I unclasp her hands. "Daniela, you're being ridiculous. I'm not leaving you."

She looks up at me, her face relaxing. We make love as if we are going to die.

☙

Heat rises from our cooling skin. The noonday star has fallen from the sky. Night throws its blanket over us. Holding her tight, I keep my fears to myself. But I know that no one belongs to another. We belong to the wind.

Later, I watch from the bed as Daniela picks up the chain and crucifix lying on the floor and grasps it in her hand.

When she is sound asleep, I make a pact with God. On my knees, I pray, "God, you can have everything but the girl."

A menacing voice responds. *No.* You *can have everything* but *the girl.*

✑

While Daniela sleeps, I creep out of our bedroom and retrieve a worn cardboard box from the bowels of the basement. It holds mementoes from my childhood in Singapore. Before we immigrated to Vancouver in 1986, my parents told me I was allowed to take only one box of belongings with me. I chose what to bring with great care. I did not pack one practical item; instead, I could not part with my memories. Sitting on the cold basement floor, I open the box and sift through photographs, love letters, postcards, seashells from distant shores, a piece of petrified driftwood, a smooth pebble found in a river bed. At the bottom of the box, I find what I am looking for: a ball of candle wax the colour of jade. As a teenager, I endured my first heartbreak by dripping hot candle wax into the palm of my hand and rolling it into the size of a walnut. I crush the ball of wax in my hand.

Spoiled

March 1996

I am a Buddhist who believes in God. I'm a syncretist, one who reconstructs or attempts to reconcile different systems of belief, fusing and blending religions, selecting from the spiritual buffet whatever seems best.

They say opposites attract. I am from the East, and Daniela is from the West. I am Buddhist, and she is Christian. Buddha and Jesus were best friends. One said "om"; the other, "amen."

When the Buddha was asked, "Are you God?" he replied, "No."

"Are you the Saviour?"

"No."

"What are you?"

"I am awake."

Me. I am too damn awake.

Throughout these weeks of sleepless nights, I feel the universe pour through me like a sieve. Merciless spiralling lights descend upon me, keeping me awake night and day. The sunshine pouring in through my bedroom window hurts my eyes. Colours intensify as my pupils dilate, giving me a throbbing migraine. In desperation for dullness, I rummage in the storage room to retrieve old paint cans and start to paint the walls a neutral white. Daniela grabs the brush out of my hand.

"I need colour in my life," she says, draping bed sheets over the windows to shield my eyes. I bury myself under the blanket. I fear I am dying a slow death. My house feels like a hospice. I am bearing witness to my own wake.

Into my third week of crippling insomnia, I am lying in bed, watching Daniela get dressed to meet a friend from graduate school. She is studying at the University of British Columbia to become a doctor. She is dressed to kill in a revealing black dress. She slips on her black leather dominatrix boots.

"Where are you going dressed like *that*?"

"To meet a friend from school."

"Is this the male friend you went skinny-dipping with at Wreck Beach?"

"I wasn't naked, you fool. I was wearing a dress."

"We were supposed to do the Polar Bear Swim together. Instead, you did it with your 'friend.'"

I turn to look at her more closely. "Are you having an affair?"

Daniela is caught off guard and falters. She hesitates before answering. "No."

For the first time since we've been together, I doubt her. Daniela slips on her black jacket and leaves, slamming the door behind her. I feel invisible, as if I am fading from her life. I am an old, out-of-style coat dangling in her closet, pushed way back among the hangers where I can be forgotten.

◌

Outside, the day is sunny and cheerful. Daniela puts on her running shoes and leaves the suite. I hear our front gate *click*.

I look for Mum in my parents' house upstairs and find her in her bedroom. She puts on a relaxation tape for me, but all I hear is garbled distortion. It sounds like the Devil talking backwards underwater. It stresses me out. I am so low. Every time I fly to the heights of heaven, I find myself plummeting like Icarus to the depths of hell, reduced to a childlike state, seeking comfort in my mother.

"Mum, I'm scared I am going to lose Daniela."

A sad smile spreads across her face, as if she knows something I do not.

"You have been with Daniela for three years now. Both of you are young, only in your twenties. Maybe you're not yet ready for marriage? Que sera, sera."

If only life were like the films my mother saw when she was a girl in the 1940s, where the boy eventually wins the girl and everyone lives happily ever after. Mum sings me her wonderful Doris Day wisdom. But a sick fear and nausea is consuming me. My life is heading for disaster and I am unable to stop it, like a witness watching the Hindenburg bursting into flames. I watch its colossal frame crashing to the ground in slow motion.

Mum strokes my hair. "You are a man now."

"Then why do I feel like a child?"

⌘

The next day, I rummage in the basement for two tennis rackets and balls. Claustrophobic in our small apartment, Daniela and I decide to go play at the courts near McSpadden Park. We need exercise. We whack the ball back and forth. It is my turn to serve. I feel a surge of pent-up aggression explode through my arm as I hit the ball with all my might, firing a shock wave of anger across the court. She lunges for the ball. The force of my volley throws her off balance. She trips and collapses. I run to her. Daniela's ankle and back have given out. She lies on the tennis court, the pavement's heat warming her torso.

"Don't just stand there. Get help," cries Daniela.

What have I done?

I run home, a block away, and summon Dad. Together we support Daniela as she limps home.

He fetches the first aid kit. Dad's profession as a medical doctor comes into good use. He wraps a tensor bandage around Daniela's sprained ankle and applies a cold compress wrapped in a towel to her sore back. He instructs her to rest.

"Make an appointment to see a physiotherapist," Dad says. "It will take time for your back and ankle to heal. Let Kagan take care of you."

⌘

Daniela is languishing helplessly in bed.

"Fuck. I feel old," she says as she crawls to go to the toilet. She must be tired of using the bedpan. The sheer indignity of being incapacitated is humiliating.

"Let me help you," I offer.

"Go away. I don't need your damn help," she says, always needing to be the independent one. And me? I am no use to her. I hand her the bedpan.

"For Christ's sake, I'm not using that again."

I am now her caretaker, and she is stubborn, cantankerous. Tempers flare, and there is a sickening aggression poisoning the air between us. We lash out at each other like an elderly couple gone senile. We are incontinent, our bodies' organs rotting: jaundiced liver, green gallbladder, black lung coughing up cigarettes.

✑

Dad climbs down the steps to our basement suite to check on us the next morning. Balancing on the stairs is now a struggle for him; his Parkinson's is a hazard. As he descends, he overhears my argument with Daniela, and in his panic to intervene, he rushes, slips on the bottom step, sprains his ankle, and lands on his tailbone.

"Dad, what are you doing coming downstairs?"

He moans as I help him back up. At the top of the stairs, I draw the line and shut the door, locking our apartment, saying firmly, "Dad, you cannot come in."

Later that night, I return from a walk and decide to check on him. I find him awake, sitting alone in the dark in the living room. An empty whisky bottle sits on the coffee table. The sight of him sitting there drunk in despair breaks my heart.

"How could you shut me out?" says Dad.

"I never meant to hurt you."

"I heard you and Daniela arguing this morning. I feel helpless. I cannot stand to see you both suffer."

I pick him up and haul him to bed. He is drunk, his body heavy with illness and drink. I try to lay him on the bed gently, but he lands on the mattress with a thud, waking Mum from a deep sleep.

"What have you done to your father?" says Mum. She gets out of bed and reaches for a robe to cover her nightgown. "This has gone too far."

CONSENSUS

April 1996

Fear, a stark white terror, turns everything cold to the touch. Daniela is awakened one morning by the sound of me dragging our kitchen table to the front door. I pile a mountain of junk there, throwing out furniture, chairs, cherished books, plants, clothes, and chipped dishes. In my anxiety I begin to obsessively clean our home. I purge myself of anything that is no longer meaningful to me. I throw out my belongings like a desperate man on a sinking ship trying to lessen his load. I want to start my life afresh, make a clean break. I hastily paint with brush *slap-slap* our front door silver to fortify our home against an invasion by the Almighty. Bargaining with a jealous God, I am willing to sacrifice everything except my beloved Daniela. Invisible forces beyond my control are pulling me in directions I do not want to go.

"Why are you doing this? Please stop," begs Daniela, forcibly taking the paintbrush out of my hand.

"Lord, you can have everything I own."

But everything is not enough. God is intractable. He whispers to me, *Blasphemer. How dare you worship Daniela more than me?*

Daniela starts crying. Hearing the commotion, Mum pokes her head out of her second-storey window to find me standing in front of a pile of my belongings in the garden. Mum shouts, "What have you done? This is the final straw."

The next day, I am waiting with Daniela and my parents to see a psychiatrist at Saint Paul's Hospital. Given my recent behaviour, my parents want a second opinion about my uncle's suspicions of my illness.

"I don't want to be here," I say.

Daniela clings to my arm. "Please, Kagan. You're not well. You need help."

The shrink appears. He leads us into his office and motions us to sit on the couch. His medical degree hangs prominently on the wall. I notice he has no framed photos of his wife and kids. Just a picture of his dog.

"My name is Dr. Cure." His handshake is hard and strong. Dr. Cure is in his fifties with a tuft of white hair and a complexion like a piglet.

Dr. Cure turns away from me. Addressing my parents, he asks, "What brings you here?"

Dad attempts to comfort Mum, but she is inconsolable. She hesitates, afraid to speak. Finally, she screws up her courage. "Kagan is behaving strangely. He has not been himself."

"What kind of behaviour has he been exhibiting?"

I am annoyed that I am being spoken about in the third person, as if I don't exist.

"He threw out all his belongings," says Mum, biting her lower lip.

"I was decluttering. Getting rid of junk I don't need."

"He threw out perfectly good furniture, books, clothes, plates, into a huge pile," adds Daniela. "I was afraid he was going to start a bonfire and burn the house down."

"Destruction of property," surmises Dr. Cure, making notes for what will become my file.

"Kagan was arrested by the police for creating a disturbance in a church a few years ago," says Dad sternly.

"The police report claims I fought with the police officers, which isn't true. But who is going to believe my word against the word of eight cops?"

"Afterwards, Kagan's uncle, a psychiatrist, suggested he was exhibiting signs of manic depression," Dad adds.

"That is most troubling indeed," says Dr. Cure, with a crease in his brow.

"He's hyperactive and can't stop talking," observes my father. He puts his arm around my mother. "He hasn't slept for the past three weeks."

"I am opinionated and have a lot to say. There will be plenty of time to sleep when I'm dead."

"So you have thoughts of harming yourself?" asks Dr. Cure.

"That was a joke." No one else is laughing.

"During the past few weeks have you felt high, elated, euphoric, or ecstatic?"

"What's wrong with feeling happy?" I ask incredulously.

"Do you feel grandiose, with high self-esteem? Like you can do anything?"

"There's something wrong with having high self-esteem? What's wrong with feeling confident?" I laugh out loud. Mum, Dad, and Daniela fidget in their seats, uncomfortable. "Yes, I have experienced all these feelings. Doc, it sounds like you are describing the positive traits of my personality. I don't know why I'm here. I'm not crazy."

"Do you hear voices?"

"I hear a voice in my head. It's my own voice, or at least I think it's my own voice. I hear your voice. I hear many voices when people talk. Doesn't everybody? I'm not deaf or hard of hearing, if that is what you're asking."

"Do you feel a special relationship with God, as if you are the chosen one?"

I look at Dr. Cure askance. "As far as I'm concerned, we are all Messiahs. Now there's something wrong with being spiritual? Then all Christians, Muslims, Jews, and Buddhists must be crazy too. With all our religious wars and people killing in the name of God, I guess the whole of humankind must be crazy."

"Do you have paranoid delusions about being persecuted or controlled?"

"God is jealous of my love for Daniela. He is trying to tear us apart."

"I don't recognize my own son," Mum sobs. Turning to me, she says, "You are not well."

Dr. Cure hands my mother a box of tissues. She wipes her tears and mouths to him, "Thank you."

"I think Kagan's uncle was correct, Mr. Goh. Kagan suffers from manic depression, also known as bipolar disorder," says Dr. Cure.

Daniela reaches out and grasps my hand. "What does that mean?"

"Manic depression, or bipolar disorder, a mood disorder characterized by alternating periods of mania and depression. 'Two poles,' with depression at one end, mania at the other end. Switching between moods is called a 'mood swing.' The course of the illness varies from patient to patient, but it appears that Kagan is experiencing an episode now, which has brought you in to see me today. I believe his condition has progressed to the point where he will need medication to regulate it."

Dr. Cure speaks but I can't hear a word of what he says. *Medication?* There is a ringing in my ears. I feel as if my head were submerged underwater.

Sound rushes in. "I'm sorry. I wish I had better news to give you."

"How bad is it, Doctor?" asks Dad.

"It doesn't look good."

Mum reaches out and clutches Dad's hand.

"Doc, you are wrong. Mum, Dad, Daniela, I've been misdiagnosed! I don't need medication. I am not crazy! I am spiritually enlightened."

Dr. Cure dismisses me. "You suffer from spiritual delusions. God ideation."

The same words Uncle Chin Chee Nan spoke years earlier. As the reality of his bleak words sinks in, my shoulders slump. My body is set in concrete.

"This mood disorder can be treated with medication, not unlike diabetes," says Dr. Cure. "Are you currently employed?"

I sit motionless. Daniela responds for me: "He's unemployed."

"Well, you will be eligible for disability benefits," says Dr. Cure. "You won't have to work."

The room is silent. We process.

Dr. Cure hands me a green soft-covered book that looks like an encyclopedia. "I'd like to give you a copy of the *DSM-IV*. *DSM* stands for *Diagnostic and Statistical Manual of Mental Disorders.*

The *DSM* is the holy bible for psychiatrists."

"So now you want to convert me to the religion of psychiatry?" I joke.

"Seriously, if you are going to live with this, I recommend you educate yourself and learn as much about your condition as possible," says Dr. Cure. "Knowledge is power."

He turns to my parents and Daniela. "I recommend that Kagan be hospitalized in the psychiatric ward for a week for his own safety."

Daniela squeezes my hand. "No, he's not that sick. Does he really need to be hospitalized?"

"It's not as bad as it sounds. Think of the hospital as a place of rest and healing, like a spa or hotel."

Without looking up from the floor, I ask quietly, "Do they provide room service?"

"The reality is, you need treatment and medication in order to get better. Otherwise, your condition will worsen."

Facing such pessimistic odds, I move from humour to hyperbole. "Maybe they should just put me in a straitjacket, lock me up, and throw away the key."

Dr. Cure raises his eyebrow, but Daniela protests. "No. He doesn't mean it. I refuse to let him be put in the loony bin."

"I could hold you involuntarily in the ward under the Mental Health Act. However, I am not going to force you to do anything against your will." Dr. Cure arranges the loose-leaf sheets of paper on which he has been writing and puts them into a crisp manila file folder. "You don't have to listen to my advice. But be forewarned, you are putting yourself at great risk."

Dr. Cure's report:

> This 26-year-old male has the usual psychological symptoms of not needing sleep, increased level of energy and speediness of thoughts. He is hyperactive, extra friendly, and amorous

and confident of himself, but rather scattered in his thinking. The patient is dressed flamboyantly in wildly clashing colours that defy conventional fashion. Extroverted, he seems to enjoy drawing attention to himself. He has an earring in one ear. His clothes are worn and torn but the subject stresses he likes his clothes the way they are. The subject makes a point that he did not deliberately tear his clothes for fashion's sake. He could be mistaken from his attire to be a street kid. He has the look of a typical bohemian artist.

Fleeting

April 1996

My father drives us home from Saint Paul's Hospital. We sit in stunned silence.

My father parks the car in front of our house. Entering the gate, I can't bear to look at the mountain of junk piled high in our garden. The wreckage looks like the destruction left in the wake of a tornado. More honestly, it looks like some madman created havoc and mayhem in the yard. That madman is *me*? I am full of remorse. Maybe Dr. Cure is right. I must be insane.

Slowly, laboriously, I carry the dining table and chairs back into the apartment. Daniela does what she can with her injury. Watching her limp as she cleans up my mess adds volumes to my dismay. One of the chair's legs is broken and it topples over when I try to balance it upright. I put my cherished books back in the bookshelves. We salvage the plants that have not been damaged. Together we gather our clothes in black garbage bags to wash later in the laundry. Daniela weeps as she sweeps the smashed dishes with a brush and dustpan. Our apartment looks like it has been ransacked. We bag the rest of the unsalvageable junk in garbage bags and dispose of them in the back alley trash can. Burdened with sorrow, we attempt to glue back together the broken pieces of our relationship.

☙

We lie in bed beside each other that night in silence. Daniela breaks the heavy tension by announcing, "I want an open relationship."

I am inert as a stone. A deep sadness wells up inside me as I stare blankly at the shadows cast on the bedroom ceiling.

Daniela continues: "Christ, I want to grow old with you. I just think we shouldn't live together. I can get my own place and we can date."

"We've come so far now only to take a million steps back. *Back where?* Open relationship. That's just a slow way of calling off the engagement, breaking up the painful way," I answer bitterly.

Daniela starts to sob. Her crying turns into wailing. She sounds like a wounded animal, as if she's been stabbed in the heart. I want to console her but she won't let me touch her. The distance grows between us.

She's just delaying the inevitable. I feel like I'm dying a slow, drawn-out, malignant death. I don't know anything anymore except I love her more than life itself. I can't live without her. I love her so much it's tearing me apart.

✑

I overhear Daniela talking to her father, Oscar, on speakerphone in the living room. "Daniela, I want you to come home. I've booked a plane ticket for you to Berlin. You can transfer your studies to a university here."

"I think I should stay with Kagan."

"Face the facts, Daniela. Kagan is sick. He is never going to get well. What Kagan has is hereditary. If you have kids, your children will have a 20 percent chance of being mentally ill. Would you want that?"

That evening, I join Dad upstairs for dinner and confide in him. "Dad. I love Daniela's parents. But their opinion of me has changed and I am no longer a desirable son-in-law. Oscar has nightmares that I will contaminate his progeny. I feel like an untouchable leper shunned by society. He wants Daniela to leave me."

Dad is quiet at first. He rests his fork on the edge of the plate and looks at me. "I understand Oscar's concerns. He only wants to protect his daughter."

I can't believe my ears. Have I no allies? I feel completely alone.

COMMON LAW

April 1996

I'm sitting in the welfare office, applying for disability benefits for the first time.

"I suffer from manic depression," I say to Mike, the man processing my file.

But all he sees is a young man trying to get a free ride, another welfare bum trying to scam the system. "Give me your wallet," he commands. Not knowing whether I have a choice, I hand it to him. He riffles through my bills, receipts, Canadian citizenship card, and library card, like a dealer shuffling a fixed pack of cards in a game called Liar. I am losing.

"What's this?" He holds up a bank card.

"That belongs to my girlfriend, Daniela. I'm running an errand for her after this."

"You live together? Then you're common law. She is your spouse. She can support you. You are not eligible for welfare."

The room is tense as he hands me back my wallet. I catch sight of a framed picture of a little white dog on his desk. It looks yappy. *What is with these horrible men and their dogs?* I ask myself. Mike loves his dog. Hates people.

When I tell Daniela the bad news, she flips. "I'm not going to support an invalid for the rest of my life!"

So this is where I stand.

God Only Knows

April 1996

Daniela is packing her bags. She has recovered from her injury but not from the damage to our relationship. She wants a better life than the one I can offer her. I don't blame her. If I had a choice, I'd leave myself, too.

Daniela hugs and strokes Tarim. Our cat purrs in her arms. "I'm going to miss you."

I watch enviously as Daniela lavishes affection upon Tarim.

Mum bears witness to this parting and tries to console us. "You hate leaving him and he hates being left behind. You are a good match."

Small consolation. *Were* a good match. As in past tense, for this no longer holds true.

Daniela slips off her engagement ring with the Double Happiness symbol and hands it back to me, placing it in my palm. By this act alone, she severs the bond between us.

She undoes the chain to her crucifix. "I want you to have this," she says as she clasps her crucifix around my neck. "I realize you don't trust God. But I want you to know that God loves you unconditionally."

She kisses me on the cheek, turns to hide her tears, and walks toward the door with her bags. "I want to be young, but with you I feel old."

She's going.

She's going.

She's gone.

The needle drops, scratches the record. It crackles with static. David Bowie sings a Brian Wilson song.

I'm sitting in the living room in the dark, lit only by a single candle flame. My vision blurs as warm salty tears stream down my face. A radiant shaft of light pierces my soul. My heart bleeds as the candle melts. Dad watches, helpless. My pain is inconsolable.

I undo the chain around my neck and remove Daniela's crucifix, placing it in the centre of the candle's flame. The gold metal turns a tarnished black. I become profane: God can burn in hell. I take the engagement ring, slip the chain through its centre, and clasp it around my neck.

❧

The knife of separation guts me. I am fighting, wrestling with myself, trying to force sleep, but it is not working. God, you have taken my sanity and Daniela. What else do I have to lose?

An alley cat screams in the night and momentarily breaks my stupor. I rush to the window and press my face against the fogging glass. Feline shapes slink in the shadows of our garden and surround our house. A female cries out in heat. Intrigued, Tarim jumps beside me to watch the drama unfold. She is also in heat, and I realize that other cats must desire her. I will not let her go outside.

I see the silhouette of a small object at our front door. Someone—*who?*—left a little toy mouse there.

My mind devises an analogy: the mouse is Daniela, and the circling cats are men trying to seduce her.

Who is fucking with my head?

I rush outdoors and pick up the toy mouse. I sniff it. It's laced with catnip and is driving the cats wild. I am certain that if I take it in the house, it will turn out to be an evil talisman. I wrap it up neatly in a plastic bag and bury it in a trash can. Running back to the house, I double-lock the door behind me, paralyzed with paranoia.

❧

I cannot sleep. I've lost track of time. It could be for days or weeks that I've been suffering from chronic insomnia. The apartment radiates the toxic fallout of our severed union. I toss and turn, curling fetal-like on the floor, shivering from a fever as my heart chakra burns.

A nauseating smell wafts through the apartment. I search for the source of the stink and find a leaking perfume bottle under the bathroom sink. In her haste to pack, Daniela left a trail of forgotten items. I toss on her school jacket, walk down the back alley, and drop the perfume bottle into the garbage can. Walking back to the house in the night chill, I put my hands into the jacket pockets. I find a condom still in its package.

Something stinks, and it's not the perfume.

"I knew it," I say out loud. "She's been cheating on me."

Inside the house, I call Daniela long-distance in Berlin.

"Guess what I found in the pocket of your black jacket? A condom. Can you explain how it got there?"

"The condom is ours. I haven't been cheating on you," she answers abruptly. "I'm not lying. Kagan? Are you still there?"

I no longer listen because I don't believe her. I hang up the phone.

❧

My solar plexus is on fire. In a semi-hypnotic state, I write Zen concrete poems that make sense only to the insane:

image
i m age
m i age
mirage
mira
image

beginner's mind
b inner mind
b inner mine
b in er mind
b in r mine
bin mine
bin in
bin
bi
in
i

EMPATHY
EMPTY
PATH

Impregnated with the seed of crazy wisdom, I am reborn a poet. I take dictation from the Divine.

❧

I can't breathe. I need to escape the claustrophobia of this house haunted with the ghost of Daniela's memory. I'm in the blazing garden, aglow with bees buzzing and the swollen, vulva-like petals of the purple irises. I am dying from heat exhaustion. The day is so beautiful, it mocks my agony. I am helpless, frothing at the mouth like a rabid dog. Mum and Dad sit with me among the wreckage.

❧

I am in the car with Mum and Dad. I look out of the window at the streets passing by and realize they are taking me to Saint Paul's Hospital. The loony bin.

Upon our arrival, Dr. Cure greets me. "You should've heeded my warning."

He instructs the male nurses to put me in a soundproof concrete room called the Quiet Room. I am locked in. Trapped. There is no way out. Alone in solitary confinement, my paranoia escalates as I watch a surveillance camera monitor my every move.

My psychic powers are omnipotent; my madness is contagious. These concrete walls quarantine my megalomaniac thoughts from contaminating mere mortal minds. If I pray hard enough, my thoughts will penetrate these walls and summon Daniela to come back to me.

The door unlocks and swings open. A heavy-set, middle-aged female nurse enters with my medication. I imagine she is Daniela many years from now. I hear the voices of Daniela's parents in my head: *Daniela is a good girl. Please, we beg you, let her go.*

I feel as if I'm holding on to Daniela so tight that I am killing her. The scales of judgment tip up and down. I have to choose who is going to live: Daniela or me. The up-and-down of the scales lessens, finally comes to a standstill. Daniela's heartbeat slows to a murmur and then stops as the nurse looks straight into my eyes. She can read my mind. The charade is over.

"Oh my God, I have killed Daniela."

The heavy nurse looms over me. Her shadow eclipses me.

"Now be a good boy." She hands me pills and a cup of water.

Her lips curl into a crooked smile as she watches me take the pills obediently.

I am mad. I am absolutely mad.

I bury myself under a blanket. I want to forget everything. My name. Who I am. I want to drown in the delirium of sleep and wake up from this nightmare.

❧

The next morning, I'm allowed to use the phone. I check my messages. "I hear you're in hospital," says Daniela, her voice monotone and cold. "What happened?"

She is alive. Daniela is all right. Thank God I am insane.

MIKE

July 1996

Approaching the welfare office, I see Mike sitting on the front stairs, smoking a cigarette. He scans the street like a vulture, picking out the riff-raff and lazy welfare bums among the respectable, hard-working, taxpaying citizens. How does he tell the difference?

By signing up for disability payments, I am aware I am becoming part of a class of people that Mike disrespects. His gaze sees only stereotypes and threatens to turn me into one. As I walk toward him, I make sure my body language says *Woe is me*, believing that welfare bums have no right to be cheerful.

As I get closer to the front steps, we make eye contact. His eyes narrow. He stubs out his cigarette on the concrete. "Where's your girlfriend?"

"She left me. Are you happy now?"

Dark Ages

July 1996

I have been home from the hospital for three months. Dr. Cure prescribed me lithium, a drug that stabilizes my moods, meaning I don't feel highs or lows anymore, just a numb flatness. Bored to death, not having to work, I spend my dull days in a prolonged Zen state of meditation learning the value of nothingness. My unstructured, shapeless days bleed into each other. I never know what day or month it is. I do nothing more important than daydream. I watch blades of grass grow and the yellow daisies sprout their fluffy heads. I blow downy tufts of dandelions into the hazy fog of my endless summer days.

One morning, I break the monotony by stepping on the scale. I recoil in horror: 238 pounds. I've gained 58 pounds. Looking in the mirror, I see for the first time what has been taking root the past three months: protruding belly, too-tight clothes, a vacant stare. I am fat and ugly, and my self-esteem is less than zero. Olanzapine. The antipsychotic drug Dr. Cure has also prescribed me is infamous for causing weight gain.

I purchase a self-help book entitled *3-Minute Abs* from a fitness store. On my way home I feel embarrassed that I've bought the book, with its ridiculous cover of a male's hard-as-steel abs. Why am I falling for all this body image shit? I should be beyond this. I resolve to try to come to terms with the way my body's changing, but it's hard to accept myself when family and friends constantly comment on how much weight I've gained.

At home, I retreat in despair and silence to my empty love nest. I sleep all day, unable to stay awake. The cruel winds tear through my vacant soul. I weep into my pillow as dust and cobwebs settle around my bed. Heavily sedated from my meds, I am more dead than alive. I cry tears of sorrow, for I have nothing today and no hope for tomorrow. I need a shaman to retrieve my lost soul, but it is gone, banished to the land of hungry ghosts.

Out the window I see a murder of crows circling overhead in an overcast sky. They land on a barren skeleton of a dead tree. The world has turned murderously medieval. I have entered the Dark Ages.

Can't stop crying
Feeling unstable.
There are days in my life
I feel disabled.
Somewhere along the way
Love died.

✑

I wake up at noon to go to the Kettle Friendship Society for lunch. I walk down Commercial Drive and head to Venables Street, where the drop-in centre offers cheap food for people coping with mental illness, addictions, poverty, and homelessness. The Kettle is the one thing that gets me out of bed every day.

On my way, I recognize a handsome twentysomething Caucasian man on the sidewalk. I see him so frequently that in my mind he's become a fixture of the Drive. I can tell from his fashionable clothes and smart appearance that he is from a middle-to-upper-class family like I am. But he paces, walks back and forth, as if he were in an outdoor psych ward. He meanders the 'hood like a stray dog without purpose, other than to kill time before it kills him. I decide to call him Stupor Man.

As I sit down with my sandwich at the Kettle, I draw similarities between Stupor Man and me. I also wander aimlessly in a cloud of gloom. I am so heavily sedated, so weighed down by my dense hangover of depression. I am wearing a chemical straitjacket—a term used to describe the use of drugs, usually powerful antipsychotics, to keep patients, prisoners, and others under care in a docile and manageable state.

I waste my days, comatose. Dreams do not provide a reprieve.

INUKSHUK

July 1996

As I languish in my bedroom downstairs, Dad wrestles his own demons upstairs. Major depression takes hold of him.

I rouse myself from bed to accompany him to Saint Paul's, where he will receive electroconvulsive therapy. Together we walk down the antiseptic, fluorescent-lit corridors, corridors I walked on my own as a patient months earlier. Today, we keep each other company as we wander through the battlefield of our fractured minds.

I feel him tremble at a pace unlike the steady shakes caused by his Parkinson's. Sensing my concern, he reassures me that the treatment will help him.

"It is not as barbaric as the movies make it out to be," he says, unconvincingly.

I wait for him in a puke-purple room on a sticky plastic seat. I wait too long. Eventually, a doctor brings him to me.

"You had one hell of an impressive convulsion," he compliments Dad.

I look at his frail body standing before me, finding it difficult to believe that, moments before, he was strapped down, teeth gritting the bit hard so he would not bite off his tongue. One thousand kilowatts of electricity jolted through his forty-watt body.

Afterwards, Dad and I walk in silence down Davie Street toward English Bay. His body is weak and our minds are tired. The bay holds the mist tight. We approach the *Inukshuk* monument: granite slabs of rock arranged to form a mighty statue of a man, a beacon of hope to those who are lost on the vast, featureless tundra. It towers over us, arms reaching out to embrace the sea like a vast father.

The sky breaks and the wind and rain pelt the *Inukshuk*, my father, and me.

I wonder, *How much pain can a person endure?*

"Dad," I say, "you are not alone."

CAN'T FORGET

August 1996

Dad knocks and enters my bedroom.

"Can I come in?"

He sits on the bed. I feel the bed sag from his weight. He pulls the blanket from my head, places his hand on my shoulder, and gently rouses me from my numbed state.

"How are you doing?"

"Fine." I rub my eyes. How can anything be fine after I've lost everything? "How are you doing?"

"Fine. Don't give up, Kagan. It's not the end of the world," says Dad. "Come on. Time to get some exercise."

He drives us to our evening swim at Templeton Park Pool. Driving is a strain on him because of his Parkinson's. I am afraid of driving. Something else I can add to the growing list of things I feel guilty about. My vocabulary is punctuated with the words *I can't*: I can't do this. I can't work. I can't function. I can't remember. I can't forget.

Dad slides the car into a disabled parking spot. We wade through the mundane sameness of our days.

I stand under the shower, enjoying the hot jet of water drumming on my brain. Even two months after my psychotic episode, I still feel lobotomized. But I am slowly reclaiming what arable peace of mind I have left. Surrounded by older naked men, I note that my body looks younger, but my illness has aged my soul. I feel old and tired. My mind has gone to seed.

We dive into the pool. Dad glides gracefully through the water like a turtle, no longer hampered by the burden of gravity and his uncooperative body. I swim back and forth across the pool repetitively, a mechanical robot.

Dullness, I tell myself, is good for me. The meditative laps back and forth across the pool free my thoughts temporarily from the otherwise ceaseless treadmill of habitual worrying that has become my life. The PA system plays soft-rock favourites on the radio. Sade's "Smooth Operator" comes on.

Suddenly, I'm drowning in a sea of liquid nostalgia.

Daniela and I are travelling in Bali, Indonesia. We are drenched with sweat and the monsoon rain. We seek shelter under an atap hut cocktail bar. We drop our heavy backpacks and a song comes on the jukebox: it's Sade singing "Smooth Operator." We start to slow dance. We kiss, kiss, kiss, we can't stop kissing. It's hot and humid and raining, but we just don't care …

I submerge my ears underwater to drown out the song.

God, I've been cheated. I've lost her forever.

I clamber out of the pool and cough up a lung full of phlegm. My eyes tear with the sting of chlorine. I mourn the death of our abandoned dreams.

Christ, we should have married. We should have had kids. We should have grown old together.

"Why is this happening to me?" I cry out loud. "What have I done to deserve this?"

LIFE AFTER LOVE

And those who were seen dancing
were thought to be insane
by those who could not hear the music.
—Proverb

August 1996

I am sitting in the back seat as my parents are driving me to Saint Paul's Hospital. Again. This is the second time in one year. I have committed no crime, but I feel like a repeat offender.

"Mum, Dad. I'm fine. I'm not sick. I don't want to go to hospital."

For a second I think of flinging the door open and running away, beating the tarmac, retreating to the streets where so many of my brothers and sisters with mental illness live in poverty. Another street kid living on the skids. But I stay, resisting the itch to run, for it would break my parents' hearts.

At the emergency ward, I go through the routine of checking myself in as a voluntary patient. Reluctantly, my parents leave, hiding their grief as best they can, until the exit door swings closed at last. I retreat to my room, burying myself under a blanket to sleep reality away.

"Wake up." I am shaken. "If you sleep, you'll never get out of here. They're watching us all the time. My name is Kevin."

Kevin is short and wears thick, black-rimmed glasses. He looks like the stereotypical nerd. He's a chess whiz. He leads me to the common room and sets up pieces on the board. "Wanna play?"

"No, thanks. I don't play competitive games." A lie. I don't know how to play and fear I don't have the mental clarity to learn a new game.

"It's not competitive. It's only competitive if you play eight rounds. Challenge someone to eight rounds, that's personal."

He tries to explain the rules of the game. I remain silent, afraid of revealing my stupidity.

The patients pace around the psych ward in boredom, walking in circles like a bunch of somnambulists. Kevin and I join them.

A woman with wild, unkempt hair standing on end as if electrified barrels into Kevin, knocking him out of her path. "Get out of my way, pipsqueak!"

A big Indigenous guy pipes up, asking me, "Why are you hanging out with that loser?"

Kevin turns to me. "Everyone picks on me cuz I'm small," he complains.

It's true. Everyone in the ward picks on Kevin, except me. I guess I am the closest thing Kevin has to a friend in here. A strong bond starts to develop between us. I am like an older brother and feel protective of him.

I can't control my dark, paranoid fear that my extreme behaviour will eventually develop into self-harm or suicide. All my notions of goodness are stripped away, revealing the sewer of shit and blood coursing through my brain. I'd renounce everything to be released from this torment.

Kevin advises me, "You must learn to discharge the Dark Side safely through art, exercise, or sports. You ever play games at the arcade?"

"No."

"You should try it. It's a great way to get rid of your aggression safely. The number one rule is: Don't hurt anybody, including yourself."

The dull days are punctuated by a bland breakfast, a bland lunch, and a bland dinner. On my third day, I join Kevin in the dining room for the first time. Prior to this, I have taken my meals in my room only.

Collecting trays labelled with our names, we sit at the table and lift their lids. *Surprise, surprise.* The same meal we had the day before and the day before that, thinly disguised as something different. Poking our food with a fork, we attempt to diagnose it.

I confess to Kevin, "I may be perverse, but I kinda like these meals. I've always liked airplane food."

"You *are* crazy. No wonder they put you in here."

Famished, I dig into the food, shovelling forkfuls into my mouth. I look up briefly to see everyone in the dining room glaring at me. No one is eating except for me. Feeling self-conscious, I lower my fork, mouth still full of food, and ask Kevin, "Why is everyone staring at me?"

"Saint Paul's is a Catholic hospital," explains Kevin. "Here, we say grace before we eat."

I am holding up dinner, preventing others from eating while they wait for me to say grace. Feeling embarrassed at my unintentional rudeness, I put my fork down and hold hands with my fellow patients. I say a prayer beneath my breath: "Dear Lord, thank you for this food we are about to receive. Bless the vegetables that were grown in the sun, soil, and rain, and the meat that was sacrificed to provide this meal. Bless the people who cooked, prepared, and served this meal. May this food bring health, wealth, happiness, peace, love, and all good things. Bless all the patients in this ward; may we recover soon and lead a balanced, healthy, and happy life. Bless friends, family, and all relations. Bless the Buddha, Dharma, and Sangha. Bless all sentient beings; may they be free from suffering. In the name of the Father, Son, and Holy Ghost, amen."

Cutlery clatters on dinner plates. We dig in.

✑

In my boredom I ride the stationary exercise bike. Going nowhere. I pace with the rest of the walking wounded, going round and round like a hamster on a wheel.

I ask a tall, ginger-bearded fellow why he's here.

He looks me in the eye and says, "Because I'm a madman."

"What happened?"

"I'm an artist. I was working on this wire-frame, papier mâché sculpture. I was spreading plaster of Paris with my hands and all of a sudden—*whoosh*." He lifts his arms like a pterodactyl taking flight. "The sirens *wooo* and then the blue and red, blue and red lights came and took me away."

The staff treats us with condescension, as if our every request is absurd. Being treated as crazy makes one crazy. The doctors and nurses joke at our expense, their laughter insulated behind plate-glass windows. They call it "gallows humour" when serious, frightening, or painful subject matter is treated in a light or satirical way. Call it what you will, but I find their jokes about the suffering of mental patients cruel, demeaning, and dehumanizing.

Anorexic teenagers, thin as skeletons, bones poking through taut flesh, push stands with saline bags *drip-dripping* into tubes stuck in their arms. Their only food. They pace round the ward, frail as ghosts.

A young Indigenous teenager named Doreen sees me writing in a journal and asks to see it. Page by delicate page, she leafs through my poems, drawings, doodles, and collages. Then she shows me her journal. Doreen must be sixteen, but she draws like a child. Wild, clashing colours scrawl across the page.

"Write me something," she says. I pick up a felt pen.

> Fortitude and pride
> as the tide subsides
> washing away
> our fears of the day.
> Usher in the stillness
> that permeates this prayer.
> Let us live in peace
> and find strength within
> when none seems there.

"That's beautiful."

Doreen makes a friendship bracelet for me. It's made of Day-Glo plastic. She slips it on my wrist next to my hospital tag.

She hugs me and won't let go.

Later, Kevin tells me she's a mother.

"Doreen's only sixteen. And she's pregnant again."

A woman named Veronica with Cruella de Vil hair scolds herself: "Get away from me, you bloodsucking vermin." She grapples with an invisible enemy, hands flailing in a manic panic, fists raining down upon her head.

I must be hallucinating. I see a purple-green-black nebula veiling her head like a storm cloud. I see every black eye, purple swollen bruise, and bloodied, stitched-up cut she's ever had on her weather-beaten face.

Kevin says, "She used to be a great beauty. Now she's a used-up crack whore. I bet you she was sexually abused as a child. All the men in her life have been assholes."

I am alarmed. Men who could not control their sexual impulses. Men potentially like me. I realize that when I'm in my manic state, my uninhibited sexual urges could become so profuse that if I'm not careful, I could go too far. The *DSM-IV* calls this "loss of insight." I don't want to become a pervert. I never want to hurt anybody. This thought scares me into sobriety.

The ward is a human junkyard filled with the wreckage of discarded lives. Kevin and I enter the TV room, where smoking is allowed. Even with proper ventilation, the room is thick with cigarette smoke and I can hardly breathe. Doreen beams at me while puffing a cigarette. The rest tease us: "Hey, Doreen, is he your new boyfriend?"

"Shut up." Doreen exhales. She turns to me. "Look at this." She stubs out the burning cigarette on her arm. Still smiling, she shows me the brand mark.

"Don't do that."

"Why? It doesn't hurt."

"It hurts me to see you hurt yourself."

A nurse pokes her head in to check on us. Doreen quickly hides her arm and the stubbed-out cigarette.

The TV is spilling forth the same old prime-time deluge of sex and violence. Doesn't the hospital staff realize that this sewage is harmful to our fragile, impressionable psyches? I turn the TV off despite the protests. Kevin turns the dial on the radio, looking for something worth listening to. He tunes in to "Believe" by Cher.

Heads bop. Toes tap. The infectious melody of the song spreads like a contagious disease. The whole ward begins to sing in unison, loud enough to wake God and scare the Devil. Veronica, Doreen, and the anorexic girls are dancing with reckless abandon, shouting the lyrics at the top of their cigarette-blackened lungs.

The inmates have taken over the asylum.

We all let loose, and for a moment,

a brief moment …

we feel normal

(whatever that means).

No, not normal.

Human.

Human again.

We do believe, Cher.

Yes.

Why?

Cuz we're living proof.

DOREEN

February 1997

After I'm discharged from the hospital, I drop in during visiting hours to see how my friends are doing. Most of the patients I know have been discharged. All except for Doreen.

I bring her flowers. Doreen is getting worse instead of better. She has put on a lot of weight because of all the heavy medications she is on. She is also now eight months pregnant, her belly bloated like a watermelon. Even though the doctors have scaled back Doreen's medications because of her pregnancy, the nurse still feeds her antidepressants, mood stabilizers, and antipsychotic drugs one by one to make sure she takes them. I wonder how these drugs are affecting her baby.

I wear the friendship bracelet she gave me. She ties a new one made of woven thread on my other wrist.

"Make a wish," she says. "When this breaks, your wish will come true."

I shut my eyes and make my wish.

✑

During another visit, Doreen shows me a home video of herself and her first child playing in a sparkling brook. The churning river is a blinding tiara of diamonds. Doreen watches herself with faraway eyes, missing her daughter. Missing the way she used to feel. She has forgotten how to smile.

Doreen rubs her swollen belly. She encourages, "Touch."

My hand touches her belly. I feel her baby kicking inside. We smile.

With each visit we have less and less to talk about, until all that is left is an uncomfortable silence. Unable to hide behind my guilt for not wanting to see her faring poorly, I stop visiting Doreen.

I wear the bracelet until, torn and tattered, it breaks off. I pray my wish has come true.

GODFATHER

October 1998

I am full after another lunch at the Kettle Society. I decide to head to Stanley Park for the afternoon. I have nothing better to do; may as well be another lost soul in Lost Lagoon.

On my way to the bus stop, I see Stupor Man. He has deteriorated. His clothes look dirty; he is unbathed. His eyes are hazed.

A voice breaks my gaze. "My God. What happened to you? You look terrible." I turn to see Peggy, an old friend, addressing me in disbelief. "I haven't seen you in a long time," she says. We hug. "You haven't been around to visit us."

Despite the brash introduction, I am happy to see her. After my diagnosis, most of my friends abandoned me. When they see me walking down the street, they cross over to the other side. When I confront them, they tell me that I am no fun anymore, my depression is a "downer," and they don't want to be around my "negativity." I've become a hermit, preferring to keep to myself. I am a shadow of a ghost disguised as a man.

"Sorry," I apologize feebly. "I haven't felt like seeing anybody since Daniela and I broke up." I avoid the other reasons.

"Not that it matters. Greg and I are getting a divorce. It's just all gone to pieces. I've moved out."

"I'm sorry to hear that."

"No need to be sorry. It's not your fault. You should visit Liam, though. You're his godfather. Promise me you'll visit him?"

My heart soars at the mention of Liam's name. Little Liam. God, I miss him.

"I will. I promise."

She pecks me on my cheek. "Be good to yourself," she whispers into my ear as we go our separate ways.

∽

As I make my way along the back lane toward home at the top of the hill, I notice a jumble of discarded toys sticking out of a trash can. I rummage through the garbage, sifting through the unwanted toys for a present for Liam. A woman appears in the backyard with her child. The mother uses clothes pegs to hang the family's laundry on a clothesline. Colourful dresses flap in the wind like Tibetan prayer flags. The young girl squeals merrily in the back garden.

I pick up a rejected blond Barbie doll, face smeared with dirt. Or is it dog shit? The cast-off doll belongs to the little girl. The mother's protective instincts kick in. Her alarm bells go off when she sees a grown man manhandling her child's old toys. She gathers her daughter into the folds of her dress, like a mother hen protecting her chicks under her wing. She covers her child's eyes, shielding her from the ghastly sight of me: an abomination, a pervert, perhaps worse. The mother grabs her daughter and carries her inside, double-locking the door.

My spirit may be wild, I may look unkempt, but I'd never hurt a child. I'd walk a thousand miles just to see a child smile. I don't blame the mother. With the shabby way I'm dressed, this is what I've become: a monster. I leave the doll and move on, feeling grotesque.

I shuffle home. The medication has given me the sensation of pins and needles in my feet, and sometimes a shuffle is all I can take. At twenty-nine years old, I relate to my father's slow, laboured gait caused by his Parkinson's.

Overhead, a flock of black crows fly home to their safe haven for the night. Home.

Up there lies ahead, the Love that I love, the Love that I love …

That old love song still haunts me. I walk up the lane silently. All I smell is garbage.

A dog barks in the distance, disturbing the peace, warning the entire neighbourhood of some perceived threat.

I am a rabid dog
barking
in the park
in the dark.
I am crazy.
I am stark
raving mad.
I will
disturb you.
I will
wake you up.
I will not
let you
sleep.
I will not
let you
rest
in peace
until
my suffering
ceases.

Lurking in the shadows
I brood,
my blood
boils
black with hatred.

⌒

While dumpster diving the next day, I find a kid's red-and-yellow plastic teeter-totter. Perfect. Up and down, up and down, up and down.

I carry the teeter-totter until I come to the picket fence of Peggy's house. I leave the toy in the garden. A token gift from a godfather who wishes he could give more. I confess I'm a lousy godfather.

I stayed away during these formative years of Liam's childhood. I was never there. Not because I didn't care. It's just that I couldn't bear to be in the presence of children, for they remind me of my aborted dreams of wanting to have a family with Daniela. The things that most people take for granted—marriage, children, family, a home—seem cruelly beyond my reach.

As I leave, I meet Liam coming home with his father, Greg.

"Hello, stranger," says Greg. "Haven't seen you for ages."

I look down at Liam, who is now a seven-year-old boy. He has golden-blond hair and a beautiful smile.

"Liam, this is your godfather, Kagan. Say hello."

"Hello," says Liam shyly, hiding behind his father. His turquoise-blue eyes burn into my naked soul.

"Go on inside now. Dinner will be ready soon," Greg says to Liam, then turns back to me. "Do you want to join us?"

"No, I have to go."

"What's this?" Liam says, his hand on the teeter-totter in the garden.

"I brought it for you," I say. "A gift."

Liam looks at his father, and Greg nods. "Thank you, Kagan," Liam says and takes the teeter-totter inside.

Before I leave, I ask Greg, "Why did you choose me to be Liam's godfather?"

"You used to have a special light. We were drawn to you."

Greg enters his house. The autumn wind scatters dried leaves at my feet. I feel the chill of winter approaching. Through lit windows I spy Liam playing with the teeter-totter in their cozy home. Then, father and son gather at the dining table to have dinner together. They bow their heads in prayer and say grace.

Poisoned

April 1999

My stomach churns, lurches me awake. I look at the clock: 3:27 p.m. My stomach churns again. I rush to the bathroom and vomit an endless flood of pills into the toilet bowl. I heave and heave and heave, throwing up years' worth of slimy green pills that have lodged in my gut, accumulating like a festering cesspool. The pills haven't dissolved as they should have. Hugging the rim of the bowl, I purge my body of the toxins.

My lips smack, my tongue rolls. I flush the toilet and wash my face and hands. Looking at myself in the mirror, I see a green ghost. My lips smack again. Not a side effect of the vomiting, but a side effect of the pills. Tardive dyskinesia, or TD, a disorder that results in involuntary, repetitive body movements. This includes grimacing, sticking out my tongue, or smacking my lips. Additionally, I can't control my rapid jerking or slow writhing movements. My tongue lolls and rolls around in my mouth, making me look like I am perpetually chewing gum or eating food. I also can't stop drooling, which reinforces the impression that I am always hungry and bingeing.

Feeling empty and absurd, I crawl back into bed in order to escape this living nightmare.

I confront Dr. Cure.

"These pills are fucking poisoning me! I'm never taking these pills again! They're fucking killing me! The meds are making me worse, not better. I feel sicker on the meds. I am nervous and anxious all the time. I can't stop shaking and trembling. I feel butterflies in my stomach."

He scribbles something in his notebook. He warns me, "You have a chemical imbalance. Bipolar is a genetic disorder. You need to take the meds; otherwise, you will get worse. If you go off the drugs, your illness will return."

"I've lost years of my life in a drugged state! Years I will never get back. I've gained so much weight I've become prediabetic. If I'm not sleeping, I'm agitated. I can't piss properly. I can't remember shit. I can't even swallow my food! The side effects of the medications are so severe that I don't know which is worse: the illness or the cure."

Dr. Cure is resolute. I leave his office fuming. My anger clears my head for the first time in what feels like years. What ever happened to the medical practitioner's Hippocratic oath, *Primum non nocere*, "First, do no harm"? Are psychiatrists exempt from taking this oath? This shrink is doing more harm than good. He is making decisions on my behalf because he believes I am not a rational human being. He will justify all his actions by saying I am so debilitated that I have "lost insight." The *hypocritical* oath in fact exonerates psychiatrists, giving them absolute power to enforce invasive interventions such as involuntary incarceration in the psych ward, forced restraints, compulsory medication, and electroconvulsive therapy. If the mental patient objects to the treatment, he or she is labelled "non-compliant" and is forced to undergo harsh interventions against his or her will. There's plenty of lip service paid to breaking the stigma and silence of mental illness. But whenever people with mental illness want to speak for ourselves and advocate for our basic human rights, we are silenced and denied the choice of whether or not we want treatment. Instead, we are locked up in mental institutions and incapacitated as disabled survivors. We are a marginalized, voiceless people, with no choice for informed decision-making.

In my fury, I almost trip over Stupor Man. He's stationed outside the grocery store at Commercial Drive and First Avenue. I reach into my pockets and toss him my last quarter.

ᔥ

Later, I gain access to Dr. Cure's report under the Freedom of Information Act. I am appalled to read, "The patient hallucinates that he has butterflies in his stomach. The patient is non-compliant with psychiatric treatment and will inevitably decompensate if he discontinues the medication. He claims the deterioration of his mental health is a result of the side effects of the drugs."

I confront him after reading his report.

"You say I've 'lost insight,' but you've 'lost' the ability to recognize a figure of speech. Your inability to understand a metaphor sounds pretty uncultured to me—"

Dr. Cure ends our session. I am overmedicated and helpless.

YOUR SADDEST CHILD

May 1999

I feel like a burden to the people who love me.

Mum. Help ... I'm lost.

From my basement suite, each night I watch Mum head to Mc-Spadden Park near our house on Victoria Drive. She paints her lips red, grabs her cigarettes, lets the front gate *click* closed softly, leaves Dad and me at home, and seeks refuge on a bench to watch the sunset alone. When she returns an hour later, I note the change in her face. Her lips are no longer red, but her swollen cheeks are.

On my way to the Kettle Society in the afternoons, I see the crushed-out cigarette butts that litter the pavement around the bench, all their muddy ends stained red. Mum bares her weakness only to the setting sun.

I am reminded of the Yiddish saying "You are only as happy as your saddest child."

LUCKY

June 1999

I meet a friend for coffee for the first time in months. "It must be heaven to be on a permanent holiday," she says to me, envious about my having so much free time. "You're lucky. It must be fun to have no job or responsibilities."

Lucky.

MANIC REALISM

August 1999

Violetta is coming. Violetta, the legendary Grande Dame of San Miguel de Allende, is coming to visit Vancouver. My brother Kakim lived in San Miguel, Mexico, for five years and used to send us postcards telling us of her infamous reputation. San Miguel is an artists' colony, a beautiful Spanish colonial town situated in the highlands, a four-hour bus ride north of Mexico City. San Miguel has attracted bohemians, rebels, renegades, hippies, Rastafarians, potheads, drunks, writers, poets, painters, actors, musicians, intellectuals, and eccentrics of all castes to her bosom. According to Kakim, Violetta is the Queen of Eccentrics.

Violetta is in her mid-nineties. She is a European who was born at the beginning of the twentieth century and has lived on five different continents and survived two world wars. A curator of a famous art gallery in Italy, she retired and settled down to live in the lap of luxury as an expatriate in San Miguel. Being fond of eccentrics, I want to meet this outlandish living legend.

"Dad, since Mum is away in Newfoundland, why don't we invite Violetta to stay with us? I'd love to hear tales about her wild past." Mum, exhausted from the caretaking of both me and Dad, needed to get away and rest and recuperate. She sought refuge in our family's summer cabin by the sea in Lark Harbour, Newfoundland, leaving Dad and me to fend for ourselves in Vancouver.

"Of course," replies my father. "Any friend of Kakim is welcome in our home. Invite Violetta to be a guest of our famous Goh hospitality."

Two weeks later, I find a postcard in the mailbox from Violetta accepting our invitation. I am so excited I can hardly wait.

Looking out the window, I see a yellow taxi pull up in front of our house. I thunder down the stairs and open the door to see an elderly woman step out of the cab. Her slim, five-foot-three frame is draped in an extravagant dark fur coat, a navy sailor's cap is tipped at an angle atop her stark-white hair, and her small eyes are magnified by the massive black glasses that command her face. Despite her frail frame, she hauls her luggage from the trunk. The taxi driver rushes to help her, but she waves him away.

"I can handle it, young man."

She tips the driver and lugs two heavy suitcases to our doorstep. I am awestruck.

"Hello. You must be Kakim's brother."

"My name is Kagan. And you must be Violetta?"

"The one and only."

She bows and takes her sailor's cap off her head in a grand sweeping gesture. Violetta reminds me of a photograph taken by paparazzi of Marlene Dietrich when she was in her nineties that I once saw in a magazine. In the photo, Marlene is shielding her face from the photographer, mortified that the facade of her former glamour has been cruelly torn away for all to see. Closer to Violetta now, I see how thin and gaunt she is under her fur coat. I can tell she used to be a great beauty. Not in the conventional sense. The sort of beauty Frida Kahlo had: the unique eccentricity of her character made her distinctly beautiful, beauty that defined her on her own terms.

She takes off her humongous dark glasses to inspect me. Her penetrating eyes burrow into me, making me feel naked and exposed.

"My, Kakim didn't tell me what a handsome young man you are."

I look down and blush. Violetta has seen nearly a century with her eyes. Nothing surprises her, for she's seen it all. She is a woman with no fear or illusions. Her stare could make the Devil blink.

"Come in." I open the door. "You'll be staying in the guest room." I lead her to the bedroom on the main floor. The room is quiet and tidy. She puts her luggage on the bed and rests her coat on top.

"How was your trip?" I ask. "Would you like to take a nap? You must be tired after all that travelling."

"Nonsense. I've travelled all over the world on my own. I have lots of energy. There's plenty of time to sleep when I'm dead."

How can so much energy exist in that waiflike body?

"Where is your dear father? I want to meet him."

"He's upstairs. He's expecting you."

We climb the stairs and meet Dad at the top of the landing.

"Welcome. Please make yourself at home. As they say in Mexico, *mi casa es su casa*."

She shakes my father's hand.

"Thank you for your kind hospitality."

"Any resident of San Miguel is most welcome in our home," says Dad. "Would you care for some tea?"

"I prefer coffee. Black with lots of sugar."

While I make the coffee, Violetta and my father get acquainted in the living room.

"How do you enjoy living in San Miguel?"

"Oh, I love it there. I wouldn't live anywhere else. Vancouver seems like a lovely city. Very clean. Unlike Mexico. The Mexicans are such a dirty people."

I flinch at the comment and sense the atmosphere shift. I know Dad won't have it. "That's an unfair comment," he says. His indignation rises at her remark. His anti-colonialist buttons are being pushed. "You are only a foreigner, an expat living in their country. What right do you have to criticize the Mexicans?"

"But I have every right. I've lived there for years. It's true. There is litter thrown all over the place. Heaps of garbage piled up high, strewn everywhere. Mountains of rubbish and no one cleans up the mess. There is no pride."

Who *is* this woman? I walk to the living room, flabbergasted, and see that Dad feels the same. He is seething, but the tense look on his face tells me he is caught between being just and being hospitable.

He tries to defend the Mexicans, but there is no arguing with Violetta. Her opinion is resolute. My father battles against this colonialist witch.

But he is losing. He has met his match in Violetta. I see Violetta spread her arms like a winged pterodactyl about to devour my father. He cowers in the corner, his head shrinking like a tortoise into its shell.

As I watch the scene unfold, I suddenly realize Violetta's true identity. She is the Dark Angel of Death come to take my father from this mortal coil. I need to put an end to this. I come to my father's rescue, standing in Death's way, preventing her from claiming him. I interrupt their conversation and gently take hold of Violetta's thin wrist. Violetta and Dad are surprised by my motion, but she follows my lead. I bring her down the stairs, and in one swift motion I open the front door, lead her to the front porch, and lock the door behind me.

"Kagan!" Her voice rings with alarm. "Let me in!"

She knocks on the door, but I hear a noise loud enough to disturb all the angels in heaven.

Death has come to take Dad's soul to the netherworld.

Visions paw at me like a cat. I resist.

Climbing up the stairs to check on my father, I find him slumped in the corner, weak and feeble.

"She is …" Dad doesn't finish.

"I know," I respond. "I'll take care of it, don't worry. Rest."

I notice a strong stench of rotting fish, as if the dead carcass of the Loch Ness monster is rotting in our apartment. The stench of dead meat is so strong it makes me nauseous. I open all the windows to air out the house.

I descend the stairs and open the front door. Violetta is smoothing out the creases in her silk blouse.

"Young man. I can't possibly stay here. Could you call me a taxi and book me into the YWCA?"

✍

I accompany Violetta to the YWCA. In the cab and still reeling, I compose a few stanzas in my head:

I can live without God,
but not without my father.

Call me a blasphemer if you like,
but the bond between my father and me is sacred.
We have so much love to deliver
before the sap in our veins dries up and withers.

If I could I would strike a bargain with Death
to let me take my father across to the other side.
In exchange I would happily give up my life
to be his constant companion.

I am jittery in the back seat. My legs are pulsating at what feels like
a thousand beats per minute. Violetta doesn't seem to notice. The
taxi is thudding down Venables Street. *A suicide pact.* It feels right.
If my father dies, I will be left without my anchor. All my life I've
been dreading the day that my father dies. As tiny colourful houses
rush past me, I make a morbid pact to commit suicide when he
dies so I can join him as he crosses the Great Divide. Violetta sits
unaware beside me.

After we drop off her luggage in her room, Violetta turns to me.
"I think you were right to separate your father and me. The conversation was too heated. Your father … I don't want to be rude,
but he is not a gentleman. You, though, you I like." She pauses,
although I say nothing. Then she declares, "It's a beautiful day."
The sky is a cloudless blue outside her room's window. "It's my first
time in Vancouver and I want to see it. Come, let us go out and play.
You will be my tour guide and show me your hometown."

If I keep Death happy, I reason, *perhaps I can make my bargain.* I decide to take Violetta to Chinatown to visit the Dr. Sun Yat-
Sen Classical Chinese Garden. We enter a moon gate to spy orange
koi fish swimming in a jade-green pool among lotus flowers.

"Kagan," she asks, "do you have a girlfriend?" The sudden
pointed question interrupts my tormented thoughts.

"No."

"A handsome man like you without a girlfriend. What a shame.
Why not?"

"My last girlfriend, Daniela, left me years ago when I fell sick. I was devastated and felt completely abandoned. As hard as I try, I can't seem to move on. I think women are scared away by my mental illness."

"What illness?"

"I suffer from manic depression."

"Ah, so that's what it is."

"What, you mean you can tell? Is it so obvious that I'm abnormal?"

"Well, there's no such thing as abnormal. But normal is boring anyway. You're just different. Unique. Eccentric. Wounded. It's not that you are a freak of nature. It's just that you have evolved. What you consider as a curse is in fact a great gift. You are special. You are perfect just the way you are."

The haze in my mind eases slightly. For a moment, the Angel of Death before me shifts back into the shape of a tiny senior in a too-big coat.

She reaches out her hand to touch a delicate purple flower with a bristly, hairy stem.

"Study this unusual flower," she tells me. "Most people would ignore this flower and think it is ugly, but I think it is beautiful. It is rare and eccentric and unique, like you and me." I look at her from the corner of my eye. She surprises me again.

"Look," she continues. "Every leaf, every flower, even the weeds are startlingly beautiful. God made everything perfect. There is no such thing as abnormal. We are all children of God, blessed with the miracle of life."

She pauses. We hear only the soft tinkle of the pond's cascading waterfall. "Normal. Hah," she says, in deep reflection. "Who wants to be normal anyway? Normal is boring. Sometimes I feel life is wasted on the living."

A robin's call erupts from behind us as the light within the garden walls shifts to dusk. This afternoon, Death has reminded me of the miracles of nature. But Death is also a hypocrite.

☙

Famished, we go to Hon's for Chinese food. I oscillate between sheer terror of this woman and keen interest. When our meals arrive, I inhale mine like a starving man.

"You eat like a prisoner guarding your food from your fellow inmates," observes Violetta. "Slow down. How do you even taste your food if you eat so quickly? Take your time and enjoy your food. Savour every morsel and it will make you immortal."

I eat slowly, feeling slightly embarrassed.

"That's better. Now, it's a shame our plans didn't work out the way we had intended. I do appreciate your invitation to come visit you, Kagan, and the gardens were very nice indeed."

I sense an opportunity. "Violetta?"

"Hmm?"

"Do you think you could forgive my father? He's a good man at heart."

"Is that what you really want?"

"Yes. Just let him be and I will be happy."

"Okay. But I am doing this for your sake and not your father's." She reaches across the table, winks, and squeezes my hand. The gesture sends a waft of her powdery perfume my way.

I accompany Violetta back to the YWCA.

"I forgot my hat," Violetta suddenly notices, feeling naked without her trusty sailor's cap. "I've had it for years! It's gone. Well, never mind; it's only a material possession. Speaking of possessions, I have a present for you."

She rummages through her luggage to find a tiny, handmade Mexican doll. The doll has braided pigtails and is dressed in a festive yellow blouse and purple skirt.

"This is your new girlfriend, to keep you company so you won't be lonely anymore."

I laugh. I am touched by her gift. "Thank you, Violetta. I will cherish this forever."

Violetta opens her arms to embrace me. I feel the paltry frame of Death's skeleton wrap around and enfold me in her cloak. For a moment my heart races, but she lets me go.

"Goodbye, young man. Take good care of your father. You are a good son."

"Goodbye, Violetta. I will never forget you."

"Of course you won't. I am unforgettable," Violetta, the Grand Dame of San Miguel, exclaims and bids me adieu. She curtsies, waves, and watches me walk down the YWCA's hallway.

⌒

Back at home, I place the doll on the mantelpiece above my fireplace. From the corner of my eye I notice an object sitting on the bed. It is Violetta's hat. Dad must have found it in the living room and brought it down while I was out. I have a superstition that whenever someone's life is spared, something is left behind as a reminder that Death has been present. I place it on my head to see if it fits. It fits perfectly. I look into a mirror to see my reflection staring back at me.

I am triumphant. I stared Death in the eyes and didn't blink.

Visions of heaven guide me into a deep slumber.

RETURN OF AN OLD FLAME

Forgetting someone is like
forgetting to turn off the light in the backyard
so it stays lit all the next day.
But then it's the light
that makes you remember.[1]
—Yehuda Amichai

September 1999

Out of the blue, Daniela sends me a letter. "Darling, sending you *bisous*. I miss you. I'm coming back to you"—my heart skips a beat, then I continue reading—"for a two-day stopover on my way to Germany."

My hopes are raised only to be dashed again, like a helium balloon taking flight just to pop. It's been three years since we broke up.

I expect us to have drifted apart, two awkward strangers with little in common but a past of broken glass. Meeting her at the arrivals gate, I feel a bittersweet refrain as she runs into my arms.

Skipping stones by the sea at English Bay, Daniela dredges up a net of memories. She tells me of her many loves who have come and gone.

"What about you?" she asks.

"I haven't been with anyone since you left."

"Why?"

---

1. Yehuda Amichai, *The Selected Poetry of Yehuda Amichai* (ebook), trans. Chana Bloch and Stephen Mitchell (Berkeley, CA: University of California Press, 2013).

"When you cheated on me, I lost faith in love. I couldn't trust anymore."

"I never cheated on you. I couldn't even look at another man. It would never even have crossed my mind."

I begin to cry. A dam breaks inside. Happy to know my suspicions were wrong and sad to have been so misled all this time.

"You were a wonderful lover," says Daniela.

"Don't say that."

I am resentful that she so cavalierly pops into my life and expects to have my attention.

Her words hurt, for I have clenched my heart into a fist, holding tight the pain of my inferiority complexes. Time has burned my anger away, but love isn't so easily resolved. I am a wounded man and do a bad job of hiding the scars.

⟡

Walking home up the back lane, she chimes, "Remember the song you used to sing for me? *Up there lies ahead, the Love that I love, the Love that I love ...*"

"Daniela, stop," I say. "I can't go back again."

⟡

The last night, Daniela wants to hold me, but I keep her at bay. Her insensitivity infuriates me. She is callous and I guard my feelings.

"How could you have left me?" I say. "I know why you left me, but *how* could you have left me?"

She bites her tongue. My wounds are still burning and my words sting. We sleep apart, heavy tension in the dark.

I have a dream. In my dream, Daniela and I are standing along the seawall. She's looking into the distance, toward the horizon of her new life, her future husband and children, whereas I feel at home here, in Vancouver, with myself, at last. I am content.

⟡

We part once again at the airport.

She's going.

She's going.

She's gone.

⊘

That evening, I take a walk around the seawall once again. The surf is pounding; salty waves spray my face. I sit down on a bench to watch the ocean's discontent.

A seagull overhead belts loudly and shits on my lap. I laugh. A message from God: *You're full of shit. Get over it.*

My Full-Time Job

January 2000

I'm sick of feeling drowsy all the time. I'm tired of sleeping my life away. I go to the bathroom, stand before the cabinet mirror, and stare into my reflection. I open the cabinet and remove my pill containers. I lift the toilet lid and seat. One by one, I pop open the containers and drop the pills into the toilet bowl. Before the capsules can sink, I push the handle and the rush of water flushes my meds down the toilet.

❧

A week later, I'm standing on the rooftop patio of my parents' house in the new millennium, staring across the skyline at the grey cityscape, lost in a haze of pollution, listening to the city drone *ooommm*. The cold winter sun is blindingly bright.

I've been awake for days. I'm thirty, but I feel like I'm a thousand years old. Now, I am dying to sleep. I have ricocheted myself to the opposite extreme: insomnia. I want to chloroform myself into oblivion, while the rest of the world is buzzing busy at work.

A new house is being erected nearby. I see it rise day by day, piece by piece, plank by plank, from the foundation up to the roof. The new model house for the twenty-first century. It dominates the smaller, older houses—reminding me that I will never own my own home, have my own family, a wife and kids, like normal people.

I see an escalator descending and ascending from heaven. The cogwheels turn and churn in a madness of productivity. And I am not riding on it. And I am not riding on it. The cast-iron heart of the city pounds *CACHUNK, CACHUNK, CACHUNK*, driving a million iron nails into my head as the day grinds away, oblivious to my existence.

All I hear is the noise of construction. Drilling, hammering, buzzing, sawing. Vultures circle, casting shadows over me, waiting for me to cave in.

I resist. I shut my ears, but the sound is coming from inside my head. The voices of the city, mocking me: *Get a job. Get a job. Get a job. Useless welfare bum. Leech. Freeloader. Get off your lazy ass and work.*

I want to shout back, *Being mentally ill is a full-time job!*

I stumble to the door of the rooftop patio, nearly fall down the stairs. I open the back door and stagger like a drunk down the back alley toward that house. I am not going to be beaten down. I won't be defeated.

God's thick finger whacks me, and whacks me, and whacks me, pushing me around like a helpless puppet. He is a merciless drill sergeant barking in my ear: "Idle hands are the work of the Devil!"

I march toward the construction site, looking for the foreman. Rolling up my sleeves, I am prepared to demand, "Give me a job, your hardest job. I'll slave and sweat harder than a thousand men. Give me a job. I won't take no for an answer. *Give me back my life!*"

I hear a meow. I look down and see Tarim. An iridescent shaft of light pierces my soul. She is in a panic, running to me. She rubs against me, hungry for affection.

Come back, she says. *It's all right.*

She rubs and rubs against me until gradually I feel the numbness give way and slowly, *shanti shanti shanti hush hush shhh shhh*, slowly, the droning stops. By small degrees, I begin to feel human again.

I pick her up and hug her fiercely. I am a balloon flapping in the wind. She is my anchor. I can feel her heart beating as I turn and walk back home. Her little black paws grip me and refuse to let me go.

DISABILITY, THIS ABILITY

January 2000

My father drives us to our evening swim at Templeton Park Pool. I am feeling sorry for my father's ailing body, sorry that the drive is hard on him, sorry for myself. He parks in the disabled parking spot and we walk together to the pool.

We dive in. Dad floats effortlessly in the water, looking content. The PA system plays soft-rock favourites on the radio. No Sade. I'm in the clear.

We swim laps, back and forth, back and forth.

Afterwards, I join my father in the steam room. Sweating away in a cloud of steam, I meet Sean, a teacher from Ireland who frequents the pool.

My *I can't I can't I can't* mantra begins. *I can't drive, I can't work, I can't function, I can't get over Daniela.* Sean listens quietly. The steam sits heavy among us.

Sean has a story for me.

"Two guys in wheelchairs meet in a pub. They have a friendly conversation. One wheels away, stands up, and does a dance to the amusement of his friends. His wheelchair act is just a practical joke. The wheelchair-bound guy watches unamused and beckons to him. The guy saunters over. The guy in the wheelchair grabs him by the collar and *beats the living shit out of him*." Sean leans in. "Never pretend to be disabled to someone who is truly disabled." He stands up, grabs his towel, and saunters out. The door slams behind him.

I am shocked. Sean has attempted to expose me as a fraud. His conviction was so strong, for a moment I question the legitimacy of my own disability.

Sean was out of line in assuming that disabilities that aren't immediately visible don't exist, but there was an element of truth to what he said. I cower in the shadows, seek refuge in my sickness, and blame society for my fears. He became sick of my self-pity, and in the hot steam, I realize I am too. I've had enough of my hard-luck stories, feeling sorry for myself, going on and on and on about my mental health.

I look at Dad. He looks concerned but remains silent. Parkinson's sends a ripple through his body. Have I ever heard him complain about that, even once? His courage moves me. To know the world, you have to embrace it. Especially on days you can't bear to face it.

Six Cups of Coffee

January 2000

An unrepentant hedonist, I've always believed "What feels good is good for you."

"Not so," says Dr. Cure, ever the killjoy. "Be watchful of becoming overexcited. Overstimulation of the senses can trigger you into an elated state of mania."

He tells me I should avoid alcohol, drugs, caffeine, sugar, dairy products, carbonated beverages, and food with colouring, flavouring, preservatives, or additives. You know, all the fun stuff in life. He says, "Everything in moderation."

I say, "Everything in moderation, especially moderation."

I let the clinic door slam hard behind me as I leave. Having nothing else to do, I decide to kill some time in the Book Warehouse across the street. Browsing through magazines, I see a coffee maker brewing free coffee, percolating in my ear. I normally don't drink coffee, but it's tempting me today. Likely because I know I can't have it. In the *drip drip* of the machine, I hear *Come on, just one cup. You'll love it!*

I throw caution to the wind and pour myself a cup, stirring in two packets of sugar and two single-serving containers of milk.

Mmm. This tastes good. So this is what I've been missing all these years. I am an instant-coffee convert. I help myself to another cup. Then another. And another. Without realizing it, in no time I have drunk six cups of coffee. The caffeine courses through my veins. My blood is mud brown and I feel great. Better than great, I feel fantastic!

An elderly woman, likely in her seventies, walks down the aisle and grabs a book off the shelf next to me. I notice the bristling white hairs on her neck and I am strangely aroused. *Pull yourself together, Kagan.*

Bursting out of the bookstore, I hurry down the busy street. I am surrounded by women and men of all ages, shapes, and colours. Everyone arouses me. My heart threatens to pound itself out of my chest. *I need to get myself home.*

I gasp a sigh of relief as I step through my front door, but the relief is short-lived. I feel as if I'm crawling out of my skin. I resist the regret I feel welling up inside me: *Why why why did I drink that coffee?* No, right now it's about survival. I make an urgent call to my father's friend Robin. Robin is in her sixties, but her spirit is young.

"Robin, how are you?"

I hear a smile in her voice. "Kagan, it's nice to hear from you."

"Can I take you out tonight?"

An hour later we are salsa dancing, drunk on sangria, at Santos tapas bar. We dance cheek to cheek late into the night.

Afterwards, I walk her home, hoping she'll invite me in.

"I really shouldn't," she says, reading my body language. "Your parents are my friends."

I arrive home in pure white agony. *She would if she could,* I convince myself. I reach for the phone. Shame and desperation battle within me. Desperation wins. I dial the number.

"Robin, you've gotta come over." I explain why in explicit detail. I think I sound convincing.

Robin pauses. A different voice responds: "Robin, don't listen to him." *Mum?* "Kagan's not well." She has picked up the other phone upstairs, concerned about how late I got home.

The shame blinds me. "*Oh my God*, Mum. Can't anyone have any privacy around here?"

Robin hangs up the phone. I stand in the middle of my living room as if suspended in rancid Jell-O, knuckling the phone to my ear.

"Kagan," Mum begins. I interrupt by hanging up the phone.

Holy shit.

It's nearly 3:00 a.m. I crawl into bed vibrating. Despite the horror I feel, the urges won't loosen their grip on me. I fall asleep, fantasizing absurdly. *Come here, baby, and pour me another cup of coffee!*

◯

I roll out of bed at noon. My mind is empty, calm, and, for a moment, without memory. I feel abstract remembrance hurling toward me like a bullet train. When it hits me, my stomach churns, and I let out a deep groan.

I climb laboriously up the stairs to my parents' place. Best to confront this like the shame: head-on.

Mum and Dad are sitting at the kitchen table. I can't read the look on Dad's face, but it's clear Mum has told him.

"Kagan," Mum says, clearing her throat. "We are taking you to see the doctor."

◯

Some days I have to remember: God is not here to fuck me over. A few days later, after I've descended into some form of reality, I'm sent to see a new family doctor, Dr. Barriers, for my Sexual Inquisition.

"Doc, I'm a virile young man. There's nothing wrong with having a healthy sex drive."

Dad interjects, "Kagan, your sex drive is in overdrive. You are not in your normal state."

"Normal. Maybe I don't want to be in a 'normal' state," I reply, shifting in my chair, feeling under scrutiny during my interrogation.

Dr. Barriers agrees. "What your father says is true. You are in a heightened state of sexual arousal. Bipolar disorder can affect your sex life, leading to a drastically increased libido during bouts of mania."

"Is that common?" asks Mum.

"Hypersexuality is found among an estimated 25 to 80 percent of all bipolar patients experiencing mania. Aside from increased sex drive, possible symptoms of mania can include uninhibited people-seeking or extreme gregariousness, promiscuity with many partners, and hypersexuality without recognition of the possibility of painful consequences. The negative consequences can be destructive and devastating."

"Is there a cure?" asks Mum.

"Hypersexuality with bipolar disorder isn't a separate con-dition or problem that needs its own treatment—it's a symptom of bipolar disorder. Once the condition is successfully treated and mood swings and symptoms are under control, these hypersexual feelings will disappear. You treat the disease, not the symptom. I recommend increasing Kagan's mood stabilizers and antipsychotic medications."

"Can you also prescribe some Viagra as well?" I joke.

"Seriously," says Dr. Barriers, "if the symptoms of mania go unchecked, it can lead to disastrous consequences."

LAURIE HALLELUJAH

February 14, 2000

I'm such a flake. I keep making the same mistake of introducing myself to women with the worst pickup line of the century: "Hi. My name is Kagan. I'm manic-depressive." I have become Joy, the woman I scorned a decade ago.

I'm an out-of-the-closet, flaming manic-depressive. I might as well have a tattoo on my forehead screaming to the world "I AM BIPOLAR!" I have no problem meeting women and getting a first date. My mistake is that I'm so honest and open to a fault that I feel I need to be upfront about my mental illness. Telling a date about my track record in the psych ward tends to kill any chance of romance. Unfortunately, most people do not find madness sexy. I keep saying to myself that the woman I end up with will not be scared away by my bipolar condition. My disclosure is a litmus test discerning those candidates who are worthy from those who are unworthy of my love. But I've been single for four years. So far it doesn't seem to be working. I'm afraid I'll be a bachelor for the rest of my life, like Cliff Clavin from the TV sitcom *Cheers*, living with my parents in my basement apartment forever. I've been single and celibate for so long I feel like a born-again virgin.

It is the first Valentine's Day of the new millennium, and I am desperate. I go through my little black phone book, calling all the single women I know, but I have no luck finding a date. Just as I'm about to give up, the phone rings. I lurch for the receiver as if it's my lifeline.

I answer, "Hello. Is it me you're looking for?"

"Ha ha. Very funny, Kagan. It's Jennaka. What are you doing tonight?"

"I have no plans."

"What? The most romantic man I know has no date on Valentine's Day?"

"Yes, I'm all dressed up and no place to go. Don't rub it in. What's up?"

"Well, your friend Jennaka is here to save you. There's a Valentine's Day poetry reading at Chuck's Pub. I know you're a poet. I thought maybe you'd like to read at the open mic."

"I don't know. I'm a closet poet. I've never read my poetry in public before."

"Then I think it's about time you made your debut. What do you say?"

"Twist my rubber arm. What the hell. Okay. I'll do it."

☙

Chuck's Pub is on Abbott Street in Chinatown in the Downtown Eastside. There's a large crowd—made up of more singles than couples, I note.

Sensing my nervousness, Jennaka encourages me: "Don't worry. You'll be great."

She gives my hand a squeeze as the emcee announces my name. I walk onto the stage and stand behind the mic. I am illuminated by a spotlight. Silhouettes stare. I clear my throat. "This one's called 'Hairy Legs.' It's dedicated to Yvonne Parent."

> My favourite street in Vancouver
> is in between Commercial
> and Victoria Drive on 6th Avenue.
>
> A lush line of Chinese elms.
> The trees, so beautifully feminine,
> wave seductively
> like a woman
> dangling her long
> > luscious hair
> as the wind makes love
> > to the air.

Their trunks
sprouting green leafy branches
remind me of beautiful women
with hairy legs.

I'm embarrassed to confess
that when I was sixteen
(old enough to know better)
sitting outdoors at Granville Island
at the Arts Club Theatre pub
with fellow poets and writers
—the riff-raff and has-beens of society—
(in other words, I was in good company)
I noticed one of my father's friends,
Yvonne Parent, sitting
with her legs kicked up on the table.

I noticed something I had never seen
on a woman before.

I leaned over
and whispered into my father's ear:
"Hey, Dad, why does Yvonne have hairy legs?"
"Oh," he said nonchalantly,
"it's because she hasn't shaved them."

Shaved?

I was so green and naive
even at that late age
I didn't realize women shaved their legs.

I always assumed
they were biologically superior.
Born genetically predisposed
to having silky smooth legs.
I was in serious shock.

Every time I glide up 6th Avenue,
I think of Yvonne
and her hairy legs.

I am in love with womanhood.
With or without hairy legs,
they sure look good to me.

A smattering of applause. I pause, wondering if the poem was inappropriate. As I step off the stage, a blond woman takes the stage next and says into the mic sarcastically, "Hey, wanna feel my hairy legs?"

Sassy. Chuckles from the crowd make me feel as if I haven't trespassed. It was a good heckle and I'm fresh out of comebacks.

She announces, "Tonight I'm either going to read my love poems or my anti-love poems. Which shall I read?"

I shout, "The love poems!"

She replies, "I'll read my anti-love poems."

Then the blond poet opens her mouth and fills my ears with spoken revelations. She's a spoken-word prophet who works twenty-four hours, seven days a week for a non-profit organization called Life. She's a spoken-word queen. She's what Coltrane was talking about when he wrote "A Love Supreme."

At the end of the open-mic readings, I thank Jennaka for inviting me.

"Congrats on your first reading," says Jennaka, patting me on the back. "I think someone wants to speak to you." She looks in the direction of the blond poet.

"Please wait for me," I say to Jennaka. "I'll be right back."

I summon up the courage to introduce myself to the beautiful stranger.

"Hi. Your reading blew me away. My name's Kagan."

"Pleased to meet you, Kagan. My name's Laurie. Laurie Bricker."

We quickly discover that we have a lot in common. Our conversation flows effortlessly. They say that people who are too similar repel, but if this isn't attraction, I don't know what is.

"Hey, what are you doing this weekend?" Laurie asks. The

question surprises me. "Do you want to volunteer as stage manager at a spoken-word event called Manor of Speaking at the Church of Pointless Hysteria?"

"What's the Church of Pointless Hysteria?"

"Two artists run it: a filmmaker named Joel Snowden and a poet named Kedrick James. They live in a huge two-storey loft in the heart of the Downtown Eastside. Joel and Kedrick throw underground after-hour 'happenings': raves, dances, art installations, and film screenings. The Church of Pointless Hysteria is an oasis of eccentricity in this no-fun city of conformity."

"Sounds like a church I can worship in. Sure, I'd love to."

"Fantastic. And there's a dress code. Make sure you come dressed in costume. The more flamboyant, the better."

☙

Tonight is our first date. Come hell or high water, I'm determined to refrain from telling her about my mental illness. I stand in front of a mirror pep-talking myself.

"Kagan, this time you will not screw up. You will purposely take your time to get to know your date. Don't scare her away with horror stories about your psychotic episodes and your hospitalizations in the psych ward. Develop a bond of trust over time. Only when she has fallen for you and you have got her hooked will you tell her about your mental illness. By then she will be hopelessly in love with you and she will accept you as you are. Remember, she is not a priest whom you need to confess everything to on the first date."

This is my strategy going into the game. This dating business is brutal and not for the faint of heart. This time I'm determined to be a contender in the World Series of Love.

I slip on my silver cowboy outfit: flashy silver pants, belt, shirt, jacket, and boots. I wear my silver cowboy hat with a blinking crystal strobe light where my third eye should be. I put on my Tibetan mandala necklace with variations on the sacred word *om*. I aim to be as charming as a prince. I look fantastic. I switch on my hat's strobe light and walk into the night to meet Laurie at the Church of Pointless Hysteria.

I meet Laurie outside. She's dressed in a pagan earth goddess costume. We beam at each other and climb the stairs up to the loft. Ambient trancelike music pounds as we enter the spacious, dimly lit loft. Tonight, the *crème de la crème* of the spoken-word scene is congregating for a night of poetic hysteria, mayhem, and madness. Everyone is dressed up in wild and exotic costumes. RC Weslowski walks around with his head inside a television set speaking in tongues. A character by the name of Mr. Fire-Man (dressed in a fiery red-and-yellow costume) is spontaneously splashing paint on a canvas. Katheryn Petersen, a.k.a. Salmon Avalanche, the organizer of Manor of Speaking, is dancing on the stage naked in green body paint and feathers, wearing a bird mask. The scene resembles a New Orleans carnival.

Laurie informs me that as the stage manager, I have to memorize the names of all the poets and performers: Shane Koyczan, T. Paul, S.R. Duncan, Rodney DeCroo, Rupix Kube, "The Svelte" Ms. Spelt, Rainy, Gabriel Martin, Kedrick James, Jen Lam, the Minimalist Jug Band, D-Noh and Deadman, Sue Cormier, and Maia Love. Throughout the night, they make me feel as if I'm being initiated into this extraordinary community. All my life the precious star of my father has dominated my night skies. But tonight, I inherit a constellation.

In the back corner of the loft, a hooded figure resembling Death sits in a space-age time capsule telling fortunes with a pack of tarot cards. When it's my turn for Death to read my fortune, I already know what the card is before he turns it over. It is the Death card.

Laurie reassures me, "Death doesn't have to be a negative thing. It can be positive. Death can mean death of ego and needy attachments. Death is always followed by rebirth. Death is part of the cycle of Samsara: suffering, death, and rebirth."

Her words resonate with me profoundly. Laurie is the distillation of every love song I've ever dug. She takes my silver hat off my head and wears it snug on hers; the hat's third eye blinks red and green like a manic stoplight. Klieg lights bathe her skin purple and orange. She's a peeled plum glistening in the sun. Being with Laurie makes me so happy, and the feeling terrifies me. I want to run out of my skin.

I am summoned by a young woman who is smiling meaningfully at me to help move a set piece. "Can I steal him away from you?"

Laurie replies, "I don't own him."

Alas, I can't help but wish she did. But instead of feeling disappointed, I choose to see that she respects that I am free, as she is free. As I learned long ago, we belong to the wind.

✑

A week later, I invite Laurie over to have dinner. Mum is visiting her family at the annual reunion of the Wong clan, and Dad has offered to make us Thai green vegetable curry, making special accommodations for Laurie, who is a vegetarian.

As Dad prepares it, Laurie and I chat in the living room. We discover we are both Virgos. She tells me she believes in angels. We empathize with each other as we discover a universe of common experiences. We read poems to each other.

After I read one of mine, Laurie says, "I feel your father's presence in the room."

I feel it too. Although he wouldn't be able to hear us from the kitchen, it feels as if his energy is eavesdropping on our intimate conversation. Knowing Dad, he's just curious to see how things are going between Laurie and me. He is sometimes overly protective of me, for he knows how hard I fall in love.

Laurie observes, "I detect your father is a little jealous of you."

Dad jealous of me? How can that be? I have often wondered whether he thinks I take for granted the advantages of youth. I am at my prime with an able body. But perhaps the real reason my father is jealous of me is because of Laurie.

Laurie is so beautiful it's almost painful to be in her presence. At the dinner table, red wine flows freely. Dad is in good form tonight, boasting about his glorious past achievements. The vegetable curry he made is delicious.

The wine bottle is almost empty when the subject of God comes up. We all express our different views. My father takes a harsh line that God is at best incompetent, perhaps even guilty of negligence. Laurie's spirituality is based on the power of the feminine shaman.

Laurie may be young, but she is wise beyond her years. My father asks Laurie about her family. Laurie tells us that her relationship with her family is one of pain, separation, and divorce. She tells us about a fiancé who abused her, beat her so bad she had to have stitches.

"But I found the courage to call the cops and press charges against him," she says. I am moved by her strength. I glance at my father and recognize the look on his face. *What a pity*, I see him thinking—wondering primarily whether Laurie, with her family history, is a good match for me. I find the judgment unfair. Something inside me shifts.

At the end of the night, I walk Laurie to her bicycle locked up in the garden. As I watch her cycle away, I hail her: "LAURIE HAL-LELUJAH! There for the love of God goes Glory on wheels!" I hear her laugh into the night.

∽

The story of Laurie's past moves me deeply. I am unable to sleep. A deep sadness wells inside me. I sit up in bed, turn on the bedside lamp, and pick up a pen and paper. I title the poem "Open Harms." *Hurt is a four-letter word …* The muse strikes me. My pen scrambles across page after page. *If I could go back in time … I'm willing to barter my soul to take your place … So you won't have a bruise on your beautiful face.* A shard pierces my chest. *Laurie.* I cannot stand to think of her suffering. The muse is leading me down a path I am unable to control, with an ultimate conclusion that becomes clearer with each word I write: *If I could I'd kiss every black bruise away … Drink in your tears for you are divine, for your joys are my joys.* Pain ripples from my chest outward, down my arms and into my hands. *Your sorrows mine … I adore you … If you chose to walk to my door, I promise I'll love you forevermore.* Love. The pain in my chest turns warm. *We will always invite love in … And shut hurt out.* The words on the page are a mess from my shaking hand. *The only four-letter word you'll ever hear from me … I love you, Laurie, truly I do.*

I am overwhelmed. I climb the stairs to my parents' bedroom and curl next to Dad in the empty spot beside him.

❧

I can't slow down my thoughts. My mind is speeding through all the red traffic lights of reason. My sadness dissolves into a fear of sleep, for I can't afford to miss out on all this precious living I have to do. Laurie Laurie Laurie. I'm so in love with life I can't sleep. I dream with eyes wide open. If I switch my mind off tonight, can I trust God to switch me back on tomorrow? My feelings are so buoyant I float upward toward the ceiling. Dad rouses himself from the depths of his sleep and holds on to me to keep me stable; I pull him along. We swing higher higher to kiss the sky to thank it for giving me this lyrical miracle sweet succulent life. Dad tries to relax me, massages my head, caresses my scalp, lifts a crown of thorns from this worrying warrior's head. Spent, he falls soundly asleep again.

I lie staring at the ceiling, my mind racing. In the slippery yolk between sleep and consciousness I see with my third eye Tarim frolicking with a white cat. It's strange to see her play with another cat, for she is usually anti-social, a snob to other cats. I have always felt sad that she is spayed. She will never be able to have kittens or enjoy sex. *Do cats enjoy sex?* I wonder. Suddenly I feel a feline presence, black sheen of a shimmering coat, crawling delicately paw by paw over me. It feels the size of a black panther. I look up, but Tarim isn't there.

I mourn my repressed sexuality. I haven't had sex since my diagnosis. I am a young man healthy in body. (I won't vouch for my mind.) I used to be virile. Now, on the increased dose of meds from Dr. Barriers, my libido is less than zero. I am in my thirties. Strong. With potential. I feel the weight of Dad's body resting directly beside me, but our bodies are worlds apart. Parkinson's has rendered his body impotent and small. *Was Laurie right? Is he jealous?*

I am suddenly bathed in a warm, vibrating, shimmering light. An angel approaches me. They are neither male nor female but both: a hermaphrodite. The angel's heartbeat penetrates me. Tears well up in my eyes as the most beautiful music fills my ears. It is the music of the spheres. The angel enfolds me in its wings. My body pulsates with a love so intense that pure sheer naked ecstasy courses through my body, illuminating my soul. I weep a river of tears as lithium capsules cascade over a waterfall.

I am holding on to the guilt of sins from days past, afraid that karmic retribution will strike me down—or, worse still, my unborn children will inherit my karmic debt. I cry out: "I don't belong!"

The angel rests on my chest, paw outstretched toward my face. They whisper in my ear: "Belong. Belong."

The angel exonerates me for my sins. God has already forgiven me long ago. I know I won't forgive myself, but for now I unclench my fists, unhand my fears, and let go into the unknown. Bliss. It is unclear whether it lasts for a nanosecond or eternity. Then, the angel's wings take flight, lifting the heaviness that plagues me.

God's Glorified Secretary

March 2000

I am so brimming with inspiration from the Manor of Speaking event and the visitation by the angel that I write forty poems in one month. I write with a vengeance, as if my salvation depended on it. I am God's Glorified Secretary pounding on the keys of my computer like Thelonious Monk. I crash my computer. Then I write by hand. Then I injure my writing hand. My muse is working me overtime to the bone with relentless intensity. I'm dying for a break from all this inspiration. I'd welcome a dry spell. Writer's block sounds like a holiday.

Of my hyperproductivity, my father says, "If you carry on like this, you'll write your whole life story in two weeks." That is exactly what I want, to lay everything down as honestly and truthfully as possible, using up a hundred thousand pens, draining oceans of ink until I arrive ... finally ... at a blank page. My pen, out of ink. My thoughts, migrated. My muse, retired. My mind, a blank expanse of Emptiness. Enlightenment is blissful Silence. Non-existence. Nothingness. I am exhausted. I need a safe haven from God's relentless gift of creativity.

One evening, unable to sleep in my delirious insomnia-induced bliss, I recall the angel's final instructions: "Share the Vibe. Share the Vibe. Share the Vibe." I think of Laurie.

I'd love to build an Open House with you, Laurie. Walk through an open door into an open room with open windows, open ceilings, open walls, and open floor. An Open House where friends and family will always be welcome to visit or stay. How will you find this

Open House? What is our address? Between the highs and lows, between heaven and hell, Nirvana and Samsara, along the Open Road you will find the Middle Path. At the end of the road, you can lay down your load and enter our Open House, our sanctuary, our safe haven, our home. In Chinese, the symbol of Double Happiness is two independent people living under one roof, but each is a pillar holding the house up together. I'll hold up one end while you hold up the other. We are all living in the same Open House with rooms of our own. Laurie, I will write you a love story. A novel so long it will take you a lifetime to finish it.

I call her the next day like a puppy dog that wants to share a special bone I've just found. In my manic enthusiasm, I don't know whether my words make sense.

"Laurie, I want to build an Open House with you, open walls and floors, between highs and lows and Nirvana, I'll hold up one end and we will live the same—"

She cuts me off. "But I'm not attracted to you sexually."

I am crushed. In an instant, I move from overinflated to spiritually deflated. I pinch the excess inches on my waist that I've gained from olanzapine.

I dare not even let hope raise its head when Laurie says, "Let's just see where it goes."

ᴏ

Depression doesn't come as I expect it to. I meditate, repeating the Buddhist mantra of non-attachment, non-attachment, non-attachment. *We belong to the wind.* These thoughts help keep my spirit buoyant. *I will enjoy this journey wherever this mighty river takes me*, I tell myself. I feel honoured to be a guest floating down this river swollen with happiness. Any attempt to force love to keep to a predetermined course will fail, for love is natural and should be as simple as a love song. I may be right, I may be wrong, but when the river pulls you to come along, for heaven's sake go when the current is strong.

ᴏ

I return to Dr. Barriers. In my openness, I tell him about my experience with the angel. He dismisses it.

"Kagan, it's called parasomnia: a hallucinatory state between dreaming and awakening, the subconscious and the conscious."

"It's a lucid state I call Dreamtime," I say.

"It's quite a common experience," he tells me.

To be made love to by an angel of pure light is a common experience? Okay … cool. More people deserve to be made love to by angels. He prescribes me an envelope of sleeping pills to combat my insomnia. He asks me to come back weekly for he wants to monitor me. "I'd just like to keep an eye on you."

Keep—an—eye—on—me? I am belittled at every turn: by Mum, by Laurie, by my shrink. But I've heard this voice of reason before. It's the Tyranny of the Rational Mind. So if I'm not rational, what am I? An aberration? Abnormal? Crazy? I think of Violetta. She was right about one thing: Who the hell wants to be normal? Normal is boring. I don't want to sacrifice my developing spirituality for the facade of "normalcy." *God, I would miss the magic!* I feel at risk of becoming another mind destroyed by the mental health system.

"You know what, Dr. Barriers? I refuse to have my spiritual beliefs desecrated, my illuminations belittled as hallucinations. That night was a spiritual awakening for me. I refuse to be medicated into oblivion. Pumped full of drugs, which make me sleep my life away. The cruel winds tearing through my vacant soul. A somnambulist sleepwalking like a ghost through the rest of my living and undying days! I don't know which is worse: the sickness or the cure. I don't want to be converted to your religion of 'normalcy.' I am happy to be crazy, unrepentantly crazy in love with this life!"

"Look, Kagan. I know these experiences feel real. But your persecutory delusions may be because of some special relationship or attribute you believe you possess, maybe involving God or some other religious figure. It's called loss of insight."

"But for the first time in a long time, I'm trusting my intuition."

"That's very dangerous for you." His voice is dry, academic, matter-of-fact.

"Who can I trust if I can't even trust my own intuition? If my reality is untrustworthy, how can I learn to be trusting? Doc, you're failing to acknowledge that there is both an ordinary state and an extraordinary state of consciousness. To one living in the ordinary state of consciousness, those living in an extraordinary state of consciousness seem to be living in a fantasy, while those living in an extraordinary state of consciousness perceive those living in an ordinary state of consciousness as living blinkered lives trapped in an illusory unreality. This schism is an illusion, for the two realities are just flip sides of the same yin-yang duality."

Dr. Barriers shifts his spectacles farther up his nose and regards me plainly. "Please make sure you take your medication each day, Kagan."

If you speak to God, it's called praying. If God speaks to you, you're fucking nuts. Am I crazy? I'm so lost. But what I do know is that I refuse to amputate my soul to fit into the grave this health-care system is digging for me. I WANT OUT!

I cycle home, reeling from the appointment. Cherry blossoms are falling like snowflakes. The spring day is bright. I am strange. I laugh when I'm sad and cry when I'm happy.

I see a park and want to lie on the grass and watch the cotton-wool clouds drift through a dome of blue. Distracted by this desire, I ram my bike into a fence and topple off. I cut my finger on a twist of metal protruding from the fence, a wide-open gash. I let out a deep belly laugh that I can't stop. The pain feels good, a welcome release. Love is the boat that keeps me afloat, and pain is the anchor that weighs me down. Red blood everywhere. *Red Rum Red Rum.* I think of the ancient doctors who used to bleed patients if their blood was too hot, to cool them off, to drain them of their demons.

Looking up, the sun glares like God's naked eyeball. His pupil dilates, taking in everything. My blood-red heart is on fire. I wheel my bike over to a table and sit down to write a poem. The wide-open wound on my finger spills blood on the scrap piece of paper I find in a garbage can. I use my blood to write a poem with my index finger. *I am a blood poet*, I think, and laugh.

O PEN
OPEN
My pen is my sword
My muse the Lord
Dressed in my own words
I disrobe
Embracing silence

I stand back to appraise the handiwork of my calligraphy as the blood dries on the page. I need to calm my raging heart-fire, or it will consume me. God wipes a lipstick smear across the face of the evening sky. I see an elderly Chinese woman practising her tai chi nearby, and her fluid movements begin to calm my soul. Wade into cool blue evening waters, merge with my reflection, soak my open wounds. I want to submerge my sorrows, disappear beneath the surface, leaving only ripples.

I cycle to Laurie's house. Seeing my wounded finger, she winces. She pours alcohol over the open wound. I look at the pale flesh of my skin and the word that pops into my mind is *Egyptian*. This is an ancient wound I've been carrying inside for God only knows how many lifetimes. Laurie wraps my finger in bandages, mummifying it.

"You know I love you, Kagan."

"I love you too, Laurie."

"But we're better off as friends than lovers. You are like the brother I never had. It would feel incestuous if we slept together."

"You're right. It's better this way. You are the sister I never had."

"You are my soul brother from another mother."

"I love you, sis. You're like ice cream. You're my favourite flavour, next to the Saviour."

She laughs, kisses me on the cheek, and hugs me. "I love you too, bro."

❧

We head to Café Deux Soleils on the Drive for dessert.

"I think I'm going to be celibate," she announces, digging into her brownie. "I want to cultivate platonic soulmate relationships with men."

I'm still a little raw from her rejection, but I reply diplomatically: "That's a great decision. I agree. It's healthy to develop non-sexual friendships with the opposite sex. There's too much pressure to sleep with your date. I'm glad we're having this conversation. Friendship is much better."

The bill comes on a tray with a couple of mints. I remember that yesterday I'd bought Chinese takeout for my parents and had kept two fortune cookies as a treat for us. I feel around in my pocket to discover the fortune cookies have been crushed. I take the pile of crushed biscuits out of my pocket and plunk it on the table. Laurie looks at me with a shocked expression on her face while I pull out the crumbly pieces from my pocket and read our fortunes out loud. We pay our bill and are about to leave when Laurie points out, "You better take that with you or you're going to offend the waitress when she takes her tip."

I wonder what she means when I look at the table to see among the crushed fortune cookies a condom still in its package. I had it in my pocket and had unwittingly pulled it out with the cookies. Laurie bursts into hysterical laughter. I turn beet red at my faux pas.

"Oops, I must be manic!"

Laurie laughs. Upon hearing me mention the word *manic*, she asks me point-blank, "Are you bipolar?"

Oh no! I've done it again. I wait for that glazed-over expression and brace myself.

"Most poets have a touch of madness. Most of my best friends are crazy too," confesses Laurie to my surprise. On our walk home, our conversation is lively and animated.

Laurie's on a different life path. I celebrate her solo flight and watch her soar free. I sing her name loudly as I cycle home, feeling a little bit free myself, too.

❧

As I prepare for sleep that night, I realize I have lost the sleeping pills. I search everywhere. Assuming they are lying at the park where I fell, I crawl into bed without them. It feels good ignoring Dr. Barriers's advice.

Tick. My watch strikes 11:00 p.m. *Where the hell is it?* Realizing the noise will keep me up all night, I tear my room apart. Nothing.

Tick. Midnight and no sign of the thing. I let out a deep yawn—sleep beckons despite not taking the pills, despite the ticking watch.

I curl into bed and grow roots into the mattress. Dreamtime greets me like a childhood friend. I hear the celestial song of a lullaby. My fears subside. The angel descends from heaven, wings beating so quietly I almost do not detect their arrival. The angel lands upon me gently, bathing me in a golden aura. I feel their heartbeat against mine. Soon, our heartbeats synchronize.

Be   Long.
Be - Long.
Belong.

As I drift into a deep sleep, I realize that the angel must have taken my pills, for I don't need them anymore. I need to spend more time in Dreamtime, away from the regulatory, ceaseless tick-tock of clocks. I let go and sleep soundly, trusting that God will switch me back on tomorrow.

Border Crossing

May 2000

"I am a father," C.R. says in disbelief. He loves Sue and baby Dawn, but there are days he has to wander alone down the railway tracks. The Road calls out to him: *Don't look back.*

One night he appears at my door looking for a friend, a place to stay. From the forlorn look on his face, I know something is troubling him. We hang out in the park, lying on the wet grass and staring at the blank sky. He smokes a cigarette as I listen to his silence.

A family of one's own. C.R. has come to see me in order to momentarily escape the one thing I want in life that I fear I can never have. This is what I am thinking as we lie there together. I turn my head to look at him. We are illuminated by a street lamp. A yellow cigarette butt hangs out of his slightly open mouth. Long eyelashes blink the night away. What he's thinking I do not know.

That night, C.R. falls asleep on the bed with his shoes on. I cover him with a blanket, but the next morning he is sleeping on the floor without it.

❧

The next night, as the sun is melting a honey liquid gold, I cycle past the Salvation Army clothes bank on Victoria and Second Avenue. I spot a gold-framed picture of two seagulls' flying silhouettes against the sun-scorched aqua-blue sky. I pick it up to get a closer look. It reminds me of a poem I have just written called "Jonathan Livingston Seagull Finds a Girlfriend" about true love and the sacred union with the beloved. I am debating taking it home—it's kind of cool, kind of kitsch—when a car whizzes by and two women yell, "Take it!"

I smile and lean it up against my bike. *Mine.*

I also find a child's plastic toy car. I think it would be perfect for baby Dawn. I slide it into my backpack, loop my arm around the picture frame, and cycle home. When I see Dawn, I see Hope. She is so beautiful, with a golden tuft of blond hair and sky-blue eyes, and the maker of the most charming squeals. When I spend time with her, C.R. tells me I'm doing "child time," as if testing the waters of future fatherhood. I know it's something I don't have to test. I want it with my whole heart. I ache as I ride into the dusk.

✑

Like the Cheshire cat, C.R. turns up everywhere. I am at the Silvertone Pub enjoying some live music when he deposits himself heavily in the seat beside me, pint in hand. Two female cellists take the stage and declare, "This is a song for a very messed-up guy ..."

The friends I am with chuckle, glance in my direction. C.R. gives me a brotherly slap on the back. The cellists mean me. I have earned the reputation of being the local lunatic on the Drive. I am East Van's resident madman.

Later, my motley crew of friends and I go to a club. We are a bohemian band of gypsies. Music pounds as if it were the heartbeat of the night. I watch C.R. with curiosity. Mania beckons. Is C.R. my best friend, my guardian spirit, or the charismatic leader of a cult? He is exorcising my demons, shouting his rhymes like a preacher of the *Old-Time Gospel Hour.* I want to leave, tear away, sever the umbilical cord that holds me to this life.

Over the music, I yell to C.R., "Life is difficult when your personality is a cult."

He yells back, "Life is difficult when your friend hands you an insult."

My karmic crimes committed once upon a time come back to haunt me. God unscrews my head, scrapes out the muck, picks out the maggots, and replants them in fertile soil. Cowering in the corner, I am a baby coughing up phlegm and amniotic fluid. I want to leave, paranoid of being initiated into a cult.

"I don't belong!"

My friends piece me back together, answering in song: "BE-LONG! BELONG!" They hold on to me tight as I lean over the abyss. They won't let me go. I give thanks for my family of friends. I am married to my friends. I am married to my community. I am married to the world. I am married to the universe. May our friendship never end. Amen.

Sunset Inn & Suites

October 2000

I am back in the throes of a bad psychotic episode. Just as I begin to feel better, I slide back here. My madness is contagious. Mum and Dad are swept away by the undercurrent of my insanity. Instead of checking me into Saint Paul's, they book a room for three at the Sunset Inn in the West End for a bit of mental health R and R.

Mum has reserved a more upscale version of the motel room she usually books for herself at the 2240 Kingsway Court Motel. When she needs to escape, she retires to a basic room for a week, brings a week's worth of groceries, and holes herself up and sleeps. For hours, days, making up for lost time. A deep sleep, dead to the world, her life, her responsibilities. During this week, Dad and I are forbidden to visit or disturb her. This time, though, the three of us pack the car and head to the West End.

I make a bed for myself on the pullout couch and lie down, staring at the popcorn ceiling.

"Mum, I am tired of constantly fighting to recover."

"Just surrender and rest," she advises me.

Fine, I think. *I will give up trying to get well and surrender into a passive state of somnambulance.* A part of me deep down knows that this is not what Mum means.

My parents lie down atop the covers of the king-sized bed and flick the television on. The heat drums. Outside, fallen leaves lie in wet clusters on damp pavement. Feeling as small as a child, I reflect on the relationships that bind the three of us.

I am so close to Dad I believe Mum feels jealous of the bond between father and son. Mum resents Dad for spoiling his sons. Dad is the softie who coddles and enables my brothers and me, whereas Mum is forced to play the role of the "bad cop." She is especially hard on me, I feel. She rarely praises me or says the words *I love you*, because the words would spoil us—and especially me, her wayward son—further.

I reflect aloud.

My words drive Mum insane. She retreats to the bathroom.

I confront her. She is sitting on the lid of the toilet seat. "Why don't you ever say 'I love you'? Why don't you ever hug or kiss me or show me affection?"

"I don't want you to depend on me. I don't want you to be weak. I want you to be strong. I don't want you to need my love," says Mum, covering her ears.

"But I am your son. I need to hear you say 'I love you.' You are my mother. I need your love, not your strength. I need to know that you love me."

Mum screams a loud shriek, like an injured animal in agony. She pulls at her hair.

I have never seen my mother in such a state.

Alarmed, I stagger. "Mum, are you all right?"

"No! You are allowed to go crazy. Your father can go crazy. Now it is my turn to go crazy!"

She screams and hits herself hard in the head with her fists over and over again. Dad and I grab her fists and wrestle her down to the ground until she stops. Mum, Dad and I embrace one another in a sorrowful heap.

SURVIVING SAMSARA

December 25, 2000

I haven't slept for several days. A bad sign, as three nights of insomnia usually triggers a psychotic episode. I am a junkie jonesing for a fresh fix of dreams to ease my frazzled nerves. I pray for sleep to descend upon me like a torrential rain, but my soul is a drought-stricken desert. I am filled with such profound sadness that I can't sleep.

I've entered a state of isolation so extreme that I've lost all sense of time. All I know is that it's around the Christmas holidays. My parents left for Mexico on Christmas Eve to take a holiday. No. Not *left*. More like *fled* for their own sanity. I chose to spend Christmas alone in prayer and meditation instead of celebrating with friends and extended family. This Christmas I am obsessed with meeting my Maker to seek penance for my past crimes. I want to pay my karmic debts so I won't have to live the rest of my life in regret.

I look in the bathroom mirror. My skin is clammy and pale. I have bags under my eyes. I grab the electric razor and shave my head. Clumps of hair fall onto the tile floor. I want to sever my past, erase my identity. I examine my reflection in the mirror, feeling my bald head. I look like a Buddhist monk on a mission of redemption. My eyes are bloodshot. I am a zombie dreaming with eyes wide open, unable to tell the difference between reality and delusion. There is no escaping the Escher-like maze of my mind.

As I sit naked, cross-legged in the darkness on the bathroom floor, my soul illuminates an iridescent green. Is this my Divine Spark leading me through the dark? Out of the shadows appears the golden Sangha: the great Buddhist patriarchs of time immemorial reflected through a hall of a million mirrors into infinity. I hear their mantras echo in unison, rising to God's symphonic celestial music of the spheres. I stand up on tiptoes, arms outstretched like a human satellite dish channelling sacred messages from God.

We are living in critical times and all souls urgently need to awaken and reach Satori, enlightenment. We children of God must awaken from our slumber and transcend ignorance. As the darkness encroaches and the end seems near, the forces of good must rise and shine as brightly as we can to become beacons guiding the lost souls back home to the light. We are all Messiahs. We must all transcend together. Our civilization is undergoing an invisible renaissance. We will transcend bigotry and prejudice when we realize that we are not alone but are All One.

The Patriarchs say, "You have an exceptional gift of compassion. You have been blessed with the ability to viscerally experience the entire spectrum of emotion. Your suffering has not been in vain."

I stand under the shooting jet of the shower head, gulping down mouthfuls of water as I undergo this holiest of baptisms.

The Patriarchs' solemn voices echo, "Embrace your Destiny. You are Enlightened. Why are you still frightened?"

Am I enlightened or suffering from an overactive imagination? Unsure how to answer the question, I open my soul wide to swallow the universe.

"Yes, I embrace my Destiny!"

The Patriarchs are swept up into a vortex swirling above me. I am left alone again in the dark shower. I blink my eyes as the stardust settles. I litter the silence with a long, tortured scream.

⌀

The next morning, my delirium ruptures long enough for me to realize that I'm out of medication. My shoes crunch along the frosted sidewalk. My breath coalesces in the crisp morning air as I walk down the street to my pharmacy. It is early, and my pharmacist, Ken, hasn't arrived yet. I begin to panic. Has his drugstore closed for Boxing Day? I try to kill time, but it won't die. To my relief, Ken appears and unlocks the door to let me in.

"Thank God, Ken, I'm so happy to see you. I've run out of medicine. You are my saviour."

I hand Ken my prescription and wait as he divvies up my pills into the blister pack. I bow in gratitude when he hands them to me. "Happy holidays, Ken."

"Take care of yourself, Kagan."

As I head toward the door, the smell of diesel suddenly overcomes me and I want to vomit. My heart beats like a wild bird trapped in my rib cage. *Did I ingest traces of diesel when I took my last pills? Did I forget to wash my hands?* The smell is coming from *inside* me. The poison spreads through my circulatory system like black tar. I wobble as if I were drunk.

Ken is alarmed. "Kagan. Are you okay?"

"No. I've been poisoned. Somebody help me."

In my panic, I stagger out of the pharmacy before I can hear Ken's response. I focus on only one thing: I need to get to the emergency ward as fast as possible. I check my pockets. Enough change for the bus. I lumber toward the nearest stop.

The bus is cold and empty. The driver is grumpy, but I don't notice. There is poison pounding through my veins. I am trying to keep it together … when I notice that only the left half of my body is affected. My right side feels completely normal.

The left side of your body is where your father's spirit resides, a voice within me says. I have always felt that I carry Dad's soul within me, the way I carry Christ and the Buddha. *And he is dying.*

Waves of terror ripple through my body. The poison is eating away my insides, but this news hurts more. I can feel him dying. I hear Dad's voice plead with me: *I'm old. I'm tired. Let me die in peace.*

I refuse to let him go. My right hand takes my left hand to comfort him. My right hand squeezes too tight. Instead of easing his suffering, I realize I am increasing it: I'm holding on to him so tightly that I'm strangling the life out of him. I can feel the life force drain from his body into mine.

I'm trying not to let my panic show. I attempt to calm myself by rocking in my seat. I look up to see two other passengers, who I didn't see board, staring at me in fright. One moves away from me to the back of the bus. I feel I'm on the verge of a heart attack. My heart chakra is an overheating engine choking black smoke.

I hit the emergency alarm. The grumpy driver screeches the bus to a halt and yells at me in protest, but I pay no mind and scramble off the bus. I see the blue and pink flicker of an Open sign in the window of a corner store. I stumble in and buy a cold bottle of water. I chug it, trying to douse the fire in my belly, but it rages out of control.

Where am I? Broadway and Burrard, okay. Okay. My eyes search frantically for a bus stop but find none. I am forced to walk to Saint Paul's on foot. I limp forward at a tortoise crawl as my youthful half tries to drag my reluctant father along.

My father is begging me to let him die. *I am tired. Let me rest.*

But I won't. I can't. I keep walking. The pain is immeasurable.

I hear God's voice berating me: *You are prolonging your father's suffering!*

I refuse to give up. I must save him. If he dies, I'll have nothing left to live for. I remember my suicide pact, and as I do, a blazing fire erupts in my left side. Dad screams in excruciating pain. I feel the impact of the searing heat. Dad protests my war with God by setting my inner liar on fire.

I labour on, crying out to the world, "They call me a liar, but I saw them set the Messiah on fire. If I was a burning house and you couldn't put me out, would you look for water in a time of drought?"

A couple out for a morning walk scurry past me in fear and disgust.

My mind is consumed by raging fire. I scream in excruciating pain. Leaning over the edge of the Burrard Street Bridge, I am tempted to jump into False Creek to extinguish the flames. I climb up onto the railing. I balance atop it, looking down. The water sparkles like a diamond tiara as I spin the roulette wheel of Samsara. I must extinguish my anguish. I turn back to see the world one last time. The bright sunny morning mocks me. It is annoyingly cheerful. The traffic flies past me, oblivious to my plight. I am one insignificant man, in an overpopulated planet of seven billion suffering souls, desiring death.

My head spins as I picture myself plummeting into the icy water. Into oblivion. I walk the tightrope in my head. One false step and I'm dead.

I feel an aching emptiness on my left side. He's *gone*.

There's nothing left of his spirit. My father, murdered at the hands of his son. I am made of ash.

I don't know how long I stand there. I slowly become acquainted with the hollowness inside me. False Creek lies in passive waiting beneath me. Life on the other side of Dad's death is quiet.

I can't bring myself to do it. *I am too much of a coward.*

Yet under the cold sun, that thought is slowly replaced with another: *I don't want to die.*

I take a deep breath and choose a different narrative: *I want to live.*

I push myself away from the railing and continue walking toward St. Paul's, drowning in my grief.

❧

At the hospital, I take a number and sit down. There is no blood, no broken bones, I am no longer shaking and yelling, and I begin to feel ridiculous sitting in the emergency ward among the visibly sick. How do we measure the suffering inside of us?

Voices torment me, tell me to run away before it is too late.

A nurse calls my number. I ask to be checked in to the psych ward. She tells me that this will be my fifth hospitalization in four years.

The voices rise to a deafening din. The nurse takes my blood pressure. The blood pressure machine is made of plastic and looks like a toy. The nurse wraps a cuff around my arm and pumps to get a reading. All of this is make-believe, a ruse, a game. I am a fraud, a hoax, pretending to be sick when I am not crazy at all.

The voices call me a liar. They warn me of the torment and pain I will suffer in hell for my sins. They mock me, insist I am only pretending to be crazy.

The nurse pricks my finger to test my blood sugar level. I feel a tiny pinprick on my thumb and see a little drop of blood pool onto the tip. She brings the inside of me to the outside. In the deep purple, I see the magnitude of my suffering. And it is as painful as a pinprick.

The voices laugh at this grand cosmic joke—and the joke's on me.

"Head back to the waiting room," the nurse says, giving me a cotton ball to press against this tiny maw of hell. "Dr. Barriers will call you soon."

In the waiting room, I look at the cover of a BC Tel phone book showing a BC ferry frozen in time. White gulls hover ahead as the ship sails the emerald seas of the Gulf Islands. Time has come to a standstill. The dust particles of the hospital are suspended in mid-air.

The dangerous side of my emotions passes. The laughter inside my head subsides to an echo that eventually abates into silence. I am neutered and feel nothing. I peer underneath the cotton ball and regard the supple lines of my fingerprint. There is no sign of the needle.

⌒

Dr. Barriers greets me in the waiting room and brings me to the psych ward.

"Do you have thoughts of harming yourself?"

"I almost jumped off the Burrard Street Bridge."

"I'm sorry. I'm obliged to inform you that you are now being held involuntarily under the Mental Health Act. The reason for your incarceration is that you pose a danger to yourself and others."

Two male nurses lock me in the Quiet Room, a windowless room so impenetrable that not even my thoughts can escape. I try in vain to slow down my anxious mind, but my thoughts bounce off the concrete walls like pinballs. The voices might be gone, but I want to ram my head against my cement cage to silence the violence within. My mind uncoils like a broken watch.

But soon I feel my Divine Spark light up an iridescent green. I am bathed in a calming glow to guide me through the Dark Night of the Soul.

Outside the door, I hear two people talking about me.

"Keep it down," a man's voice says. "Some of us are trying to get some rest."

Have I been noisy?

I overhear a woman's voice say, "He's really lost his mind. Try to meditate to discipline your rebellious mind."

Nurses would never give instructions through an unopened door. I realize that these two must be fellow patients. I am convinced that they have read my mind; they have overheard the battle I have been waging with God over the domination of my father's soul. I must be in a really bad state if my fellow patients consider me mad.

I sit cross-legged. My mind glows opalescent. *Is this enlightenment or madness? Am I a Buddha, God, or just extremely odd?*

I sit in darkness. I am still so very far from the shores of sanity. In solitude, it sinks in. I have killed my father. Patricide: the greatest sin.

A janitor enters my cell. He mops the floor and wipes the stainless-steel toilet clean. His movements are quick and brisk, as if he's nervously cleaning a lion's cage. He is so near I can smell his fear. I wonder whether he's ever been attacked by a patient.

"Don't be scared. I won't hurt you. I may be crazy, but I'm not dangerous. I'm a man. Not an animal." But he leaves before I can utter another word.

A nurse enters and gives me a handful of pills and a cup of water. "Take these. They will help you sleep."

Sleep. I want an escape from this living nightmare. I pop the pills in my mouth and swallow them back with the water. I lie down, curled up in fetal position, and let the dark overwhelm me.

Some immeasurable time later, I'm shaken awake. A nurse beckons me out from the Quiet Room to a phone. It is a long-distance call from my mother in Mexico.

"Hello?"

"Kagan. Are you okay? I am coming back as soon as I can."

"Mum, is Dad okay?"

"Yes, he is here. Do you want to speak to him?"

"Yes, please."

"Hello, Kagan, are you all right?"

"Dad, is that you?"

"Yes. How are you doing?"

I can't believe it. He is alive. Thank God, he is still alive. I am mad. I am absolutely mad. Never before have I been so glad to be mad.

◌

I'm moved from the Quiet Room into a bed in the general psych ward. The patients' beds are separated by curtained partitions. I close my curtains for privacy. My bed is next to a window, letting in white light from the moon.

A mousy woman peeks from behind my curtain and asks, "May we come in?"

She and her tall, bearded companion saunter in before I have a chance to answer.

"My name is Mary." She takes my hand. Her hand is soft and warm. No calluses. Without being invited, she sits on the bed beside me.

"And I'm Gerry," the man says. I recognize the voices as those that spoke to me from outside the Quiet Room door. Gerry's hair is standing on end, as if he were electrocuted at Science World. I recognize Gerry from my previous visits here. He is a permanent resident.

"You shouldn't fight with him," says Mary.

"With who?" I ask.

She hands me an envelope. Inside is a Get Well card. I open it and read:

LIAR LIAR

Mary sees right through me. Is my truth a lie, or am I lying about the truth? My mind is playing tricks on me. I can't trust my instincts, because my hallucinatory reality is false. Why did I imagine that I had killed my father? I try to make sense of what has happened. I set fire to my inner liar to find among the ashes a diamond of truth.

"Turn it over," says Mary. I flip the card to see:

You can hide the truth from yourself. You can even lie to yourself, but you can't hide anything from God. God was testing me, casting a dress rehearsal to prepare me for my father's inevitable death. He challenged my suicide pact and taught me how my unhealthy attachment to Dad causes suffering. The suicide pact was a narrative that I needed at that moment; I had to know that there was a way I could extinguish my suffering. But today I stared into the Abyss and chose life over death.

"Do you know why we have come?" says Mary.

"Yes. I have blasphemed against God. I have been battling God, cursing His name in vain for inflicting me with this incurable affliction. Me. An unrepentant blasphemer. A born-again sinner."

"Why are you angry with God?" asks Gerry.

"How can I trust a cruel and vengeful God?"

Mary says, "God is incapable of hate. His love for you is unconditional."

I clasp my hands in prayer. I grip so tight, my knuckles turn white. Mary takes my hands in hers. I break down, sobbing. Gerry smiles warmly. The two of them wrap their arms around me. I hug them back.

◌

The next morning, I curl myself into the corner, scared of my fellow inmates who roam the corridors shouting, grappling with their hallucinatory demons. I am finally on the other side, and right now I need distance.

I anxiously chew my fingernails until they are raw. A kind nurse wraps Band-Aids around my fingers to prevent me from biting my nails. When she is gone, I unwrap two of the Band-Aids and paste one horizontally and one vertically on the window to form a crucifix. Nothing is familiar in this hostile environment except the sun streaming through the window. As the afternoon sun sinks lower in the sky, its brilliance floods the room through the refracted section of the window's glass. It showers me with a billion tiny rainbows. Overwhelmed, I lay down my arms in surrender. The light recedes from the room, retreating through the window from where it had come. My war with God is over.

I have my whole life ahead of me. What am I going to do? I can't spend the rest of it in and out of the hospital. I can't be dependent on my parents forever. This is no way to live.

After the Dark Comes the Light

December 29, 2000

Mum and Dad book the first flight home they can, but it will be a few more days until I see them. I pass time quietly in the ward, reflecting. They are anxious to see me, but I know the time apart is good for me.

C.R., Sue, and baby Dawn drop in to visit. It is so good to see them. I feel normal in their presence. They make me laugh and forget my troubles in this horrible, oppressive ward. Their genuine, down-to-earth friendship makes me feel human again. It's been ages since I last smiled and laughed this hard.

They stay until visiting hours are over. I walk them out, reluctant to see them go. Big bear hugs. C.R.'s shoes *click-clack* on the linoleum floor. He tap dances, does the shuffle. Pulling out his harmonica, he blows a few bars. The inmates are digging it. He flashes me a shit-eating grin à la Jack Nicholson in *One Flew Over the Cuckoo's Nest*. Nurse Ratched comes storming out, afraid the disturbance will rattle the other patients. I am banished to the Quiet Room.

I am in trouble with a capital *T*. Damn C.R. has got me in the hole. I smile. It's worth it.

❧

After the hole, I feel cramped, stunted, like my whole psyche needs a stretch. I get down beside my bed and settle into child's pose. I breathe deep. My hips are storing centuries of stories. I breathe into them.

I remember when my friend Bryan Phillips talked to me about

meditation a few weeks back. We were at the park, and after listening to my woes, he recommended it to me. Afterwards, I picked up a book by Jon Kabat-Zinn called *Full Catastrophe Living*, which explains how mindful meditation can help medical patients with chronic pain and stress. I breathe in slow through the nose, count to five. Hold the breath for five. Breathe out through the mouth, count to five. I shift my body into downward dog.

Looking up, I see Mary sitting on the floor across from me. She observes me curiously and arranges her limbs into a good-enough version of downward dog. I hear her exhale loudly. As I look down toward the floor and float my right leg up, a big grin stretches across my face.

◑

Later, I am on the rooftop of Saint Paul's Hospital. The nurses let me out with a pass for a breath of fresh air, up here where the sky is blue and pigeons fly free, away from the antiseptic corridors, fluorescent lights, and linoleum floors reeking of Lysol. Sitting in this oasis Zen garden, watching sparrows splash in a pond teeming with goldfish, I meditate in a shaft of sunlight, drunk on the rapture of being alive.

Rebirth

January 2, 2001

My parents rush into my hospital room, looking wary.

"Have you slept?" I ask, concerned. I am sitting on my bed, washed, neatly dressed, and calm. A world apart, I realize, from what they were expecting. Relief ripples through them like a warm gun.

Mum kisses me on the forehead. I stand up, collect my things, and we head for the door. I feel Dad tremble beside me and I grab his arm to help steady him. Mum takes Dad's other hand and we exit Saint Paul's in this way together.

The first thing I do when I enter my suite is draw open the curtains and throw open my windows. I air it out. Fresh air and light. I feel like a wildflower germinating through the cracks of concrete. I look ahead to regeneration and renewal.

RUNNING IN THE FAMILY

April 2001

I have spent the past three months delving into alternative healing, exploring tai chi, qigong, yoga, and shiatsu massage. I was looking for something that would cure my condition, but I've realized there is no one magic remedy for it. Making my health my first priority means making lifestyle choices that will enhance my well-being. I keep a wellness journal and start consciously writing down all the practices that help me manage my condition. Through this process, I understand that seeing a psychiatrist regularly and taking my medication diligently are crucial. Nonetheless, I still feel something is missing in my life. I can't deny that Western clinical treatment can play an effective role. However, I feel that Western medicine alone does not seem to offer holistic improvement in mental health consumers with a long-standing or chronic history of mental health issues. I have spent hours researching meditation, qigong, yoga, laughter yoga, cognitive therapy, diet and nutrition, self-acupressure massage, dance therapy, and exercise as complementary treatments to mental health. I realize I have bitten off more than I can chew: mastering all these modalities will take me several lifetimes! Even so, I feel I am at the brink of something important.

I lace up my running shoes and head to the racetrack near Templeton Community Centre. Through the process of reflection in my wellness journal, I have learned that jogging is one of the best things for me.

I work up a good sweat, lungs inflating and deflating like a balloon. The red sun cools into an evening of lavender blue. The air is crisp. Pink cherry blossoms burst into fullness. The clenched fist of winter relaxes; the flowery splendour of spring unfurls. Season of rebirth, transformation, and change.

Ahead of me on the racetrack is a young Chinese girl riding her tricycle. I try to pass her. She won't let me. I try again. She stays stubbornly ahead of me. This girl has spunk in her.

She reminds me of the stubbornness that I had when I was her age. I would often jog around the park near my house. One day a man in his twenties came running up behind me. I made up my mind that, come hell or high water, I would not let him pass. We ran ten rounds. Both of us worked up a sweat, but still I would not budge. If he sped up, I'd speed up. My stubborn determination was an inexhaustible reservoir. Defeated and panting for breath, he asked me, "Kid, how old are you?"

Old enough to run you into the ground!

The young girl is still ahead of me, pedalling away. She shimmers like a mirage beyond my reach. Yes, she runs me into the ground. Attagirl!

A strange premonition comes over me. I wonder whether she could be like my future daughter. She has my same dogged determination. Suddenly I become self-conscious of my weaknesses.

Would I want my future children to see this side of me?

❧

Returning home inspired, I begin something that has been on my mind for weeks. I have been following Kabat-Zinn's program at the stress reduction clinic at the University of Massachusetts Memorial Medical Center closely, and I decide to create a series of Mental Health Stress Reduction Workshops myself.

I write a proposal. I draft a series of workshops that focus on yoga, diet, massage, laughter therapy, mindfulness, and dance therapy. I make photocopies and slip into the mailbox envelopes addressed to the Kettle Friendship Society, the Coast Foundation, the Mood Disorders Association, the Canadian Mental Health Association, and the Vancouver Richmond Mental Health Network. Then I wait.

STUPOR MAN

May 2001

I feel good. I feel in control. I feel like I *want* to be in control. I see that my parents are proud of me. And I am proud of me too.

In contrast, I watch over the months as Stupor Man becomes dirtier, shabbier, and more dishevelled. He no longer bathes. He doesn't change or wash his clothes, which eventually become worn and torn, the cuff of his pants ragged. His handsome face turns sullen and sunken, stubble growing into a tangled beard. A long shaggy mane replaces his once neat, well-groomed hair. He loses weight, looking emaciated. He has become one of the walking dead. His shadow has more life and substance than he does.

I feel guilty for thinking this, but I want to distance myself from him. He reminds me of my own past wretchedness. His youth has drained out of him like air out of a punctured tire. He is going no-where but downhill.

One day I notice that his shoelaces are untied. They are trailing along the ground, getting filthy from the street. He has given up, lost all hope, and doesn't even care to tie his shoes. My pity quickly evolves into embarrassment, disdain, then disgust. I am awash in intense hatred toward him; his decline strikes too close to home.

I want to walk up to him, grab him by the collar, and shake some sense into him. "Wake up, man! You don't need small change. You need to change! Don't you realize your shoelaces are untied? If you don't tie your laces, you're gonna trip and fall. Then who's gonna pick you up? For goodness' sake, pick yourself up. Don't let yourself go to pieces and fall apart. If you fall on the streets, people will step on you. They won't just step on you; they'll kick you when you're down. The meek won't inherit the earth. Instead, they'll be trampled and stepped on, ground down, and crushed by the wheels of commerce and progress. You must fight to survive in this cruel, merciless world."

I want to slap some sense into him. I want to save his life.

Instead, I avoid him, walk by like just any other stranger.

Eventually, he stops walking up and down the Drive. One day he is there, the next day he disappears. I search for him, but I never see him again.

But I remember him. I'm aware of how easily I could have stood in his shoes. I wish I had retaught him how to tie his own shoelaces.

PRIDE

June 2001

There is interest in my proposal, but a staff member of the Vancouver Richmond Mental Health Network gives it to me straight: my idea is ahead of its time. Nonetheless, something tells me not to be discouraged.

For now, I decide to channel my energy into volunteer work instead. After witnessing Stupor Man's decline and disappearance, my need to give back to my community becomes overwhelming. I feel genuinely in my heart that I have something important to give.

I hear from a friend that the Coast Mental Health Clubhouse is looking for help. Initially, I volunteer as a receptionist manning the phones. Later, I am encouraged by the Coast staff to enrol in an employment program for the mentally ill and disabled called Fast Track.

I am paired up with a Fast Track employment worker so she can help me find work. She reads the job postings to me in a deliberately slow and loud voice, making the assumption that I am illiterate. I am offered jobs as a dishwasher, as a street cleaner, and handing out free newspapers. All the jobs are menial and minimum wage. When I inform her that I have a university education, she is surprised and labels me "high functioning." When I tell her that I graduated from Ryerson Polytechnic University, where I directed an award-winning film, and that I want to continue making films, she says that I am being too proud, unrealistic, and "grandiose" in my ambitions.

"Here's the thing," she says. "Most of the individuals here are so incapacitated by their illness that they have forgotten how to do the kinds of activities that are routine for most of us."

Her words insult me. Is this my new normal?

But I want progress. Not only this, I also want Mum's approval.

I take a busboy and dishwasher position at the Salt N' Pepper Bar and Grill. I have to carry heavy trays of food, clear the tables, and wash dishes. Within the fast-paced environment of the restaurant, I note how much the sedative effects of my medication slow me down. I feel like I am moving in molasses. The manager criticizes me for being too slow; then he criticizes me for being slow and stupid. Off my game, flustered, and feeling incapable from his comments, I drop a heavy tray of dishes that smash, splinter, and scatter across the floor. The boss fires me on the spot. I lasted three days.

The worst part, though, is telling Mum. I have let her down. I have let myself down. I can't even do a simple job as a busboy and dishwasher. I feel like a failure, a loser.

But Mum surprises me when she says, "A first step taken by a long-bedridden accident victim is a major success. You have gone through a long haul of bad years. To me, your job as a busboy is a major success and a major step. That you have the courage to defy conventional thinking regarding 'good' jobs and start at the bottom—that takes courage. Now the only way you will go is *up*. The other day, I went to an optician's to fix my spectacles—I sat on them! The optician was an Iraqi from Kuwait, who had left Kuwait during the war, leaving his home and three cars, and arrived penniless in Canada. He had been a banker before the war and had a good life. In Canada, he had to start over again. He worked first in a factory minimum-wage job, then as a taxi driver. He now owns a house and a business. This is a man who once had everything and then lost it. But he was a man who had enough pride in himself not to care about starting all over with a minimum-wage job. That took courage.

"I realize that there has been some tension between us the last few months. But I was overwhelmed, Kagan, and feeling awful. I do have faith in you. I believe that you can do anything you put your mind to. I am proud of you. I love you very much."

SPOKEN REVELATIONS

March 2003

I spend my days volunteering, reflecting, and writing. I am taking care of myself. And as the years go on, I realize more and more how important the arts are to my journey of recovery.

As an initial form of self-therapy, I start to write about my feelings and experiences of living with a mental illness. I perform at open mics, readings, and festivals, and on radio. My reputation as a mental health advocate and activist leads to my being dubbed with respect "the bipolar poet laureate" by my peers.

Shortly after reading "Hairy Legs" at Chuck's Pub in 2000, I read my first short story, "Joy," at Black Sheep Books. When I say, "People with mental illness must be stronger, braver, more street-smart just to get through the day," a young woman in the audience cheers, "Yes!" After the reading, she approaches me and introduces herself as Angel. She says she realizes from hearing my reading that she too has a bipolar condition but has been in denial until now. She has been suffering from mental illness since her teens. She tells me that my reading has helped her recognize and come to terms with her diagnosis. With her permission, I recommend my psychiatrist to her, whom she has been seeing ever since. She is now stable, on medication, and leads a productive, balanced, and happy life as a dance student.

Months later, I read at the World Poetry Reading Series at the Vancouver Public Library. A woman comes up to me after my reading and asks whether she can purchase a copy of my manuscript. I sell my book to her. Later, I receive an email from her. She tells me that she is a psychiatric nurse, but when she herself is diagnosed bipolar, she loses her job and her husband divorces her because she is now "useless."

On another occasion, I decide to premiere my recently completed short story "Life After Love," an account of one of my stays at Saint Paul's, at Bukowski's—a pub that hosts a spoken-word open-mic night called Tales of Ordinary Madness. A woman of South Asian descent in her twenties named Farah is onstage. She takes off a wig to reveal her bald head. She then strips naked and dons a blue hospital gown and slippers. She announces to the audience that she has just discharged herself from Saint Paul's Hospital's psychiatric ward and calls herself "a freak, loony, lunatic, crazy, nuts, psycho, insane." She announces loudly, "I am bipolar, manic-depressive." She is clearly psychotic, and the audience is freaked out by her bizarre behaviour. I ask the host whether I can read after her. Once she leaves the stage, I read my short story "Life After Love," dedicating the reading to her. She listens attentively and cries during my reading. After the reading, you can hear a pin drop. The woman embraces me, and we hug for what seems like an eternity. A beam of healing light bathes us, shining down from above.

I have not only witnessed first-hand the power of art to heal but also benefited from it myself. As I sift through the pages of my wellness journal, noting the ups and downs since my last trip to Saint Paul's in 2000, I see how my journey to wellness is a delicate balance of self-discipline and self-love. There is choreography to my journey, a slow dance back and forth.

THE MENTAL HEALTH
STRESS REDUCTION
WORKSHOPS

January 2005

Have the times caught up with me yet?

It's a new year. A time of rebirth, regeneration, and renewal. Feeling bold, I mail my proposal for the Mental Health Stress Reduction Workshops once more to the Vancouver Richmond Mental Health Network, this time addressing it to the coordinator, Ron Carten. He receives it with enthusiasm. Ron gives the project the green light. I've been given the opportunity to make my dream a reality.

As the project coordinator, I search for what I call peer mentors—mental health consumers/survivors who have found creative ways of managing their condition and have expertise in various health fields—to facilitate the workshops. Through my own efforts and those of the Network, I gather together an extraordinary group of individuals: Glen Pavlick will teach mindfulness meditation; Patrick Michael will workshop diet and nutrition; Sarah Toolan will teach yoga; Bob Krzyzewski will teach do-in massage and qigong; Dave Macintosh will facilitate workshops on laughter yoga; and Rose Ananda Heart will teach dance therapy.

Our varied visions align under a single aim for the workshops: we wish to help empower the mental health consumer by providing safe, well-tested healing modalities. Empowerment is emphasized because we hope the skills that are taught will foster greater independence and self-reliance, boosting self-esteem and optimism.

The goals of the workshops are to teach prevention, intervention, and recovery skills to mental health consumers, establish a peer support group among mental health consumers, and create a safe environment to explore mental health issues and emotions.

The Mental Health Stress Reduction Workshops are a dream that came true. We run seven free workshops between March 14 and May 2, 2005, at the Gathering Place and the Mount Pleasant Neighbourhood House in Vancouver. They are a great success. They are ahead of their time because they emphasize the *health* aspect of the various wellness programs offered within mental health organizations. In the decade to come, I will watch as such programs become well established and are offered more frequently within the mental health system.

The peer mentors become some of my dearest friends. Many go on to careers facilitating workshops. For instance, Glen establishes mindfulness meditation classes at the Coast Clubhouse, and Sarah works for the Vancouver Richmond Mental Health Network teaching yoga to mental health consumers/survivors.

I believe that if one has the right intentions, the right resources will manifest because the universe is abundant. The journey from idea to manifestation has been an extraordinary one. The Mental Health Stress Reduction Workshops were a convergence of like-minded souls, a coming together of community for the purposes of empowerment, bonding, and healing. They reminded me, after so many years of hopelessness, that with patience and determination, dreams can attain fruition.

Colony Farm

If you bring forth what is inside you,
What you bring forth will save you.
If you don't bring forth what is inside you,
What you don't bring forth will destroy you.
—Gospel of Thomas

November 2006
I am being driven to Colony Farm, a forensic psychiatric prison for the criminally insane. The road to the prison is rugged with muddy potholes, jostling the car's suspension. Muriel is pensive, puffing on a cigarette as she drives me to visit her son, Daniel. She normally doesn't smoke, hasn't for years, but her son's dire circumstances have driven her to pick up the habit again. I roll down the window for fresh air and breathe in the smell of the wet, wild, grassy field. As the car approaches the maximum-security prison, I wonder how on earth my friend Daniel could become so violent.

Daniel assaulted his girlfriend during a psychotic episode, kicking her in the head with his steel-toed Doc Martens boots until he fractured her skull. Their three-year-old son witnessed this horrific act of violence. His girlfriend survived but will be traumatized for the rest of her life. The forensic police were summoned, and Daniel ended up imprisoned at Colony Farm.

Although Daniel was one of the most narcissistic people I had ever met, I didn't think he was capable of *this*. I was in shock when I heard the news. Is there a place for forgiveness in a situation like this?

Daniel is an artist, painter, writer, poet, philosopher, and self-proclaimed prophet of the Downtown Eastside. He has a Messiah complex because he resembles and is often mistaken for Jesus by the drug addicts, alcoholics, prostitutes, and other residents of East Hastings. He used to belong to a religious cult called the Golden Dawn but has since defected. To call him a prolific writer would be an understatement. At the age of twenty-six, he has written forty-nine manuscripts of prose and poetry.

Daniel and I once lived together as roommates. He used to record his stream-of-consciousness thoughts, ideas, conversations, and inner monologues with a mini-cassette recorder. He would keep me awake as he recited freestyle poetry into a microphone amplified by a speaker late into the night. Daniel adopted a stray cat from the street, which ending up having fleas. I had an allergic reaction to the flea bites, but he refused to deflea his cat. It was either the fleas or me, so I moved out, despite having nowhere to go.

We didn't speak for years. One day, I bumped into Daniel with his girlfriend at the Under the Volcano Festival of Art and Social Change at Cates Park. His girlfriend had just given birth to a baby boy. Daniel then told me he had been diagnosed with paranoid schizophrenia. His past behaviour suddenly made sense. In light of this new understanding, we mended our friendship. He half jokingly and half seriously called me the Bipolar Buddha and himself the Schizophrenic Christ.

Outside the car window I watch different-coloured rabbits in a field. They hop about freely on the prison grounds, in view of the inmates' windows. The walls of the prison create more boundaries than just the material.

Muriel parks, and we approach the heavily guarded prison gates. The prison guards check our IDs and conduct a body search. Surveillance cameras observe our every move. The entrance is a double-locked door. A prison guard enters the security code, and the door unlocks. Once cleared, Muriel and I walk down the maze-like network of corridors. Finally, after much effort, we find Daniel sitting alone in the TV room, staring vacantly like a zombie at the images on the screen.

"Hi, Daniel, how are you doing?" I ask, sitting down on the chair next to him. I realize how stupid and inane the question must sound to him. I think back to all the empty questions I used to have to field from friends. He remains silent, heavily sedated by medication. Finally, he breaks the silence.

"I can blame what happened on my mental illness. But I've had a lot of time to think about what happened. I must take responsibility for my behaviour, no matter how horrible my actions were. I've been doing a lot of soul-searching to come to terms with this. It's taking me all my courage and strength to admit this."

Daniel has the stare of someone who has found the ugly spirit in the mirror. He does not flinch from the truth. He is a shell of a man, but I nonetheless see that the truth has set him free. No prison walls can cage his soul.

I slip off my Buddhist prayer bracelet from my wrist and give it to Daniel as a token gift of friendship. He hugs me. He holds on to me until I have to go.

❧

The drive away from Colony Farm with Muriel is silent. She chain-smokes; I roll the windows down.

I recall something my father said to me after I wrote the poem "Nothing Is Forged Without a Fire." In the poem I differentiate between the "good" insane and the "bad" insane. I condemned criminally insane individuals like Charles Manson, Ted Bundy, and Robert Pickton. At the time, I needed to draw a line between "us" and "them." Yet Dad said that I should have compassion for the criminally insane. At the time I could not fathom being compassionate toward the Mansons, Bundys, and Picktons of the world. I refused to feel compassion for sociopaths who feel no remorse.

But now I realize that Dad was right. Dad is the closest person I know to have attained Buddha nature. We ought to feel compassion for Manson, Bundy and Pickton because their souls will suffer in the hell of Samsara for eternity. However, having compassion for them does not mean forgiving or exonerating them.

I also feel compassion for the other types of criminally insane individuals. Over the years, I have been researching the status of the mentally ill throughout the continent. In the United States, thousands of people with mental illness are imprisoned for crimes they committed when they were mentally ill. Many of them are on death row or have been executed for the crimes they committed when they were sick. They are sick individuals who need treatment and rehabilitation—not mere punishment. Perhaps if they were given the opportunity for treatment, they too could discover their remorse and come to terms with their illness. And perhaps this would also give those who were hurt by the criminally insane the chance to heal.

How do you forgive someone who has committed an unforgivable crime? I glance at Muriel. One hand balances a half-burnt cigarette on the steering wheel and the other grasps the gear shifter so tight her knuckles are white. Her cheeks are wet. I rest my hand on her right hand and give it a gentle squeeze.

Maybe you can't forgive. But compassion, if you can find it, will heal.

ADVOCATING FOR MYSELF

February 2007

My eldest brother, Kasan, has come to visit from England. I haven't seen him in several years. I feel obliged to update him about the living hell I have suffered. I regale him with accounts of the numerous manic, psychotic, and depressive episodes I've endured. It's been seven years since my last visit to Saint Paul's, but in my warped perception I still focus on it as if it were yesterday. I use it to define my character. When I finish assaulting him with my horror stories in the psych ward, my brother asks, "Why do you define who you are by your suffering?"

I am taken aback by his question. I am expecting the usual reaction I get from friends and family: glazed-over resignation and helplessness or sympathy and pity. Kasan, on the contrary, will not let me wallow. Instead, he dishes out a fair measure of tough love. I normally would have been defensive, but my brother's question disarms me because it comes from a place of genuine caring, compassion, and concern. I realize he is right. I am actually taking pride in being a victim and survivor of the mental health system, blaming society for my misfortune. I am proud of having survived and suffered the way a veteran is proud of having fought in the Great War, wearing his medals on his chest as proof of his bravery and valour, except the Great War I have been fighting is in my head. The Great War I have been fighting is with myself. The Buddha says attachment is the cause of suffering. In my case, I have become attached to my suffering. I've been living by the motto "I suffer, therefore I am." I was institutionalized and have inadvertently accepted the label of professional mental patient. And I'm sick of it.

There is, in fact, much to be proud of. I focus so much on the horror, but I have been making steady improvements. On this night, I vow to break my attachment to the suffering of my past. I choose to create a different narrative.

In the next weeks, I realize that I have allowed myself to become a passive victim of psychiatrists who are well-meaning but don't take the time to really listen to or address my complaints of being overmedicated or sedated into a comatose state. I take matters into my own hands and switch psychiatrists.

My new psychiatrist, Dr. Phillip William Long, advises me to get off lithium because it is ineffective in treating my bipolar condition. Initially, I am wary of doing this, thinking that the drug is my only lifeline to keep me stable. But it obviously isn't working. Dr. Long says that there are other options, alternative medications that can be more effective. He puts me on Epival (also known as divalproex), an anticonvulsant used to treat epilepsy, because it has been proven to be highly effective in treating bipolar disorder. He also puts me on a low dose of loxapine, an antipsychotic medication. Slowly but surely, the meds help to stabilize me. I no longer suffer from extreme mood swings.

I discover that psychiatry is not an exact science. At best, psychiatrists make an educated guess based on the signs and symptoms they observe in their patients that help them determine a diagnosis. It takes a lot of trial and error and experimenting with different drugs before an optimal balance or equilibrium is reached with an effective concoction of medications, a process that is often painful. But the key to recovery nonetheless starts with self-advocacy. One must speak out against prescribed medication that is ineffective or that results in side effects that feel worse than the illness itself.

Six months later, I discover the Wellness Recovery Action Plan (WRAP) in a book entitled *Winning Against Relapse* while browsing at Odin Books, a mental health bookstore. WRAP, a program developed by Mary Ellen Copeland, teaches me wellness strategies and skills in crisis prevention, crisis intervention, and post-crisis recovery for mental health. I no longer feel like a passive victim of my unpredictable mood swings. WRAP helps put me in the driver's seat. I learn to regain control of my life. I learn wellness strategies that help me prevent relapses. I now not only know what triggers my episodes (like sleep deprivation, chronic insomnia, marijuana, alcohol, extreme stress, and trauma) but also have the strength to avoid these triggers, and I know what steps to take to alleviate symptoms as they arise. WRAP changes my life for the better. I am so enthusiastic about it that I eventually work as a WRAP facilitator, co-facilitating workshops at North Shore Psychiatric Services at Lions Gate Hospital in North Vancouver.

And I don't stop dreaming.

Out of the Woods for Good

Because of WRAP and achieving balance through the right concoction of medications, I have been symptom-free and have not had a relapse for more than sixteen years. I feel like I've been given a second lease on life. But despite these improvements in my mental health and the overall quality of my life, I still feel anxious and apprehensive.

Steve Keary, a long-time friend and neighbour of my family, says something to me that finally hits home: "Kagan, you keep looking over your shoulder waiting for the other shoe to fall. The suffering you endured in the past is finally over. You can stop worrying whether or not you're going to relapse or be hospitalized. Don't worry. You're out of the woods for good."

It is true. My life has turned the corner. I *am* out of the woods for good.

After my stint as a WRAP facilitator, I trained and worked as a peer-support worker for Early Psychosis Intervention. I then went to Douglas College to train as a community social service worker. Through my practicum, I eventually got a job as a mental health worker at the Kettle Friendship Society drop-in centre—the very same one I used to use as a client. Eventually, I began working at the society's housing centres, and now I work at Kettle on Burrard, a sixteen-storey apartment building housing 140 residents. I have been working for this outstanding organization for more than twelve years now.

I consciously try to be a good role model by treating the residents I serve with courtesy, respect, dignity, kindness, and compassion.

I try to model good behaviour, and I've noticed my efforts seem to be working, as if there is a chain reaction, a trickle-down effect, where the residents reciprocate by treating the staff and their co-tenants with more kindness, courtesy, and respect. I genuinely care for these residents.

I often think about Dr. Cure's comment that people who have mental illness, especially people with bipolar conditions, typically do not work. He told me point-blank that I would never work for the rest of my life. For years I believed him. But I'm living proof that he's wrong.

I recognize that life is a never-ending process of making mistakes and making amends. To quote a Japanese proverb, "Fall down seven times. Get up eight." I still feel the occasional tremors, but they're nothing compared with the seismic earthquakes that used to devastate me.

Recovery is a process too. It begins before any kind of diagnosis or epiphany about your situation, and it never really ends, but it plateaus once you learn the tools and skills that can help you achieve a certain level of stability. *Recovery* does not necessarily mean *cure*. One does not always return to normal. Oftentimes, recovery means coming to terms with a "new normal"—finding meaning and purpose in one's life even if things will never be the same again. It is crucial to be patient with yourself; recovery can take a long time and has its challenges. You must acknowledge the small successes as well as celebrate the big ones.

I want to take this opportunity to say two things to my fellow mental health survivors. The first is to encourage you to make your health your most important priority.

My life became manageable and easier once I made that decision.

I put my artistic career before my health repeatedly throughout the early aughts, and as a result I had relapse after relapse. An often-quoted definition of insanity is to do the same thing over and over again and expect a different result. Art is good for me in that it gives me a goal and a purpose in life, but it is not good when I sacrifice my health in the pursuit of my artistic career. It was only when I made my health my first priority—even before my loved ones, my family, my career, interests, or anything else—that I realized I have a choice to live a healthier, happier, saner, and more balanced life.

The analogy I give is that of a train. My health used to be my last priority, an afterthought—the last carriage in a long train being dragged along with struggle. My health is the engine placed at the back of the train, pushing all the other carriages forward with great effort, friction, and resistance. Once I put my health at the front of the train, as the engine of my life, where it rightfully belongs, it pulls all the other compartments forward in the right direction, moving easily and smoothly with momentum. Once I make my health my first priority, everything falls into place. I am healthier, sober, saner, and happier while practising my art.

In other words, you must emphasize the *health* aspect of mental health. Too many mental health consumers/survivors lead unhealthy lifestyles, including taking recreational or street drugs, abusing alcohol, smoking cigarettes, drinking too much coffee, consuming too much sugar, and eating an unhealthy diet of junk food. I want to encourage mental health consumers/survivors to focus on improving their health by exercising regularly, practising healing modalities such as meditation and yoga, abstaining from abusing drugs and alcohol, and eating a healthy and nutritious balanced diet. With good health, what seems impossible becomes possible.

Second, mental illness is not necessarily a curse or a cause of suffering and hardship. The media oftentimes projects bad news about people with mental illness, portraying them as dangerous and violent. This is a misconception, for most people with mental health challenges are peaceful and harmless, and are more likely to be the victims of harmful violent abuse or assault by others. We need to counter this imbalanced negative perception with their success stories; they can be positive, contributing, and responsible citizens of society, and they can be artists with heightened levels of creativity, spirituality, empathy, and compassion. When people with mental illness undergo tremendous suffering, it awakens empathy and compassion for others who suffer too. Mental illness is neither entirely negative nor entirely positive. Like the yin-yang duality of life, mental illness delicately balances both. I want to contribute to turning a negative impression into a more holistic one.

I used to identify myself as a mentally ill person. However, we are not our diagnosis. When a person has cancer, we don't say, "That person is cancer." I'm not a sick person, but rather a person living with a sickness. I am first and foremost a person. I am also a son, brother, husband, cousin, uncle, friend, artist, filmmaker, author, poet, playwright, actor, mental health advocate, and activist.

The *illness* aspect of mental illness is only the tip of the iceberg. Much hidden potential rests beneath the surface. I refuse to call manic depression or bipolar a "disorder" or an "illness." I prefer to call manic depression a "condition," for it has the potential to be a tremendously positive force in one's life. In my life, I try to harness this untapped source of creativity and spirituality not just to survive, but to thrive. I turn this curse into a blessing when I learn to embrace this all-too-human bittersweet condition called life.

CODA: LOVE LOST AND FOUND

In late 2009, Mum almost dies of a vascular aneurysm. After her surgery, the doctor tells her nine out of ten patients with her condition do not survive. She is lucky to be alive. A week after her attack, her husband is admitted to the same hospital for aspiration pneumonia. She is on the tenth floor and he a floor below on the ninth. She is worried he would defy the doctors and nurses and storm the ward to see her. I am the only son of their four who lives in Vancouver. I hold the fort, communicating with my brothers on the phone, keeping them abreast of the latest developments of Mum and Dad's ailing health.

Two months later, Dad passes away on January 10, 2010, from Parkinson's disease. His name, Goh Poh Seng, means Precious Star in Chinese. My father—so in love with life. The legacy he left our family—his beloved wife, Margaret, and his sons, Kasan, Kajin, Kakim, and me—was to savour and cherish the preciousness of life.

Two years later, my mother is diagnosed with terminal pancreatic cancer. Most patients live only a few months after this diagnosis, but Mum outlives all the doctors' predictions and lives more than a year, a few months longer than expected. I attribute my mother's longevity not only to her resilience but more so to her determination to focus on life instead of her impending death. She chose to surround herself with only positive, happy, and affirmative friends and family, and shunned those who felt sorry or pity for her coming demise. In the end, my mother died gracefully, drifting peacefully into the ether of the netherworld on March 2, 2013.

I mourn the death of my parents with intensity, but I survive it.

One day shortly after Mum's death, I bump into my friend Salman Husein on Commercial Drive. He introduces me to his friend Julia Hogeling, who, unbeknownst to me at the time, will become the most important person in my life. A year before, Salman had invited Julia to the world television premiere of my documentary film *Stolen Memories* at the W2 Media Café. I didn't meet her that night, but on the Drive she tells me she liked my film. *Stolen Memories* took me fifteen years to complete; it was one of the hardest things I had ever untaken, and the standing ovation at the premiere was one of the high-water marks of my life. I am touched by her comment.

I am struck by Julia's demure beauty and grace. She has auburn-brown hair, sparkling blue eyes, and the biggest, most radiant smile of anyone I have ever met. Her smile enchants me. I immediately fall in love with that wide grin. Teeth perfect and white like in a toothpaste commercial. She is special. A miracle. A revelation. If I kiss her smiling lips, will her infectious happiness spread to me?

Salman acts as matchmaker. He asks Julia, "Do you think Kagan is kissable?"

She answers with an enthusiastic "Yes!"

Julia and I go for our first date on June 11, 2013. We go to the Fifth Avenue Cinemas to see Richard Linklater's film *Before Midnight*. After the movie, I walk her to the Burrard SkyTrain station. When I do kiss her for the first time on the corner of Georgia and Burrard, she beams a smile so radiant and blinding I imagine it stops traffic.

I am so keen to see Julia again that I arrange to meet her the next day for our second date, once again at the Fifth Avenue Cinemas, to see *The Kings of Summer*. Afterwards we walk to the dog park at Kits Beach and kiss under the dying rays of the setting sun.

Julia and I start to date. She is unlike any woman I've ever been with. I usually go for the "moody artist" type, but Julia is a preschool teacher. I worry at first that we won't have much in common, but what I discover with her for the first time in my life is a sense of calm, peace, and happiness. I eventually learn that Julia *is* an artist—an artist with kids. She is the Frida Kahlo, Emily Carr, and Georgia O'Keeffe of children: a child whisperer. She has this special ability to encourage, nurture, and bring out the best in a child's nature.

We move in together into a one-room studio suite in the West End with our cat, Minu. Having been an East Van boy, I am not used to living downtown with my West End girl, but I soon grow to love living near beautiful English Bay and Stanley Park.

I want to take Julia to the most romantic town I have been to, so in 2014 we visit San Miguel de Allende. During our stay, and without Julia's knowledge, I have a jeweller custom-make two sterling silver rings with the symbol of Double Happiness. I ask the jeweller to have our names engraved on the rings. I arrange for Julia and me to take a hot-air balloon ride. We get up at five in the morning and drive to a field at the outskirts of town. My amigos Paul and Serge fill the giant hot-air balloon with helium. Julia and I climb into the basket. Paul lets go of the ropes tied to weights that hold us to the ground. We slowly float into the sky. The balloon rises higher and higher until we have a bird's-eye view of San Miguel below. Julia and I hold each other and watch the sun rise over the horizon. It is here that I pop the question. She is taken completely by surprise. She says yes, and I slip her engagement ring onto her finger and ask her to slip my engagement ring onto my finger. We create our own traditions.

We have a small wedding ceremony on November 8, 2014, at the Historic Joy Kogawa House in Vancouver, where I have been the writer-in-residence for four months. We say *I do* dressed in traditional Chinese attire in front of an intimate crowd of forty guests. On July 26, 2015, we hold our second wedding ceremony at the Strathcona Community Gardens, where we celebrate with a larger group of friends and family. Julia and I walk arm in arm down the aisle of trellised grapevines. Miniature disco balls hang from the ceiling of the walkway. We come to a round pond with lotus flowers and lily pads. The pond is teeming with koi fish. Salman is our best man. He presents us with our wedding rings. Julia and I say our wedding vows and kiss in front of our family, friends, and relatives when the marriage commissioner says, "I pronounce you husband

and wife. You may kiss the bride."

Our reception is held at Trout Lake Community Centre. Friends and family give speeches and perform at an open-mic talent show. Everyone contributes to a potluck dinner. We dance late into the night. I am certain I am the happiest I have ever been. I survived Samsara; now I am thriving in Nirvana.

ACKNOWLEDGEMENTS

I am eternally grateful to my publisher, Vici Johnstone, and to Sarah Corsie (editorial and production), Malaika Aleba (marketing and publicity), and Meg Yamamoto (copy editor), of Caitlin Press for championing my work and publishing this book. The hard work, dedication, patience, and perseverance paid off with the end result of a book we are all proud of publishing. I hope this memoir helps to break the silence of the taboo of mental illness by expanding the conversation on mental health from a consumer/survivor's point of view.

Special thanks to my amazing editor, Holly Vestad, who expertly wove these thematically linked separate short stories into a seamless chronological narrative. Holly got into my psyche and preserved the poetry, hypomanic witty wordplay, and lyricism that are integral to my identity and persona as an East Van Commercial Drive bohemian spoken-word poet Mad Artist. Holly has an uncanny empathetic and intuitive understanding of the subject matter of mental illness. I was privileged to work with her on the substantive edit, which was one of the most rewarding collaborations I've ever experienced with an editor.

I dedicate this book to my family: my beloved wife, Julia Hogeling-Goh; my father, Goh Poh Seng; my mother, Margaret Joyce Wong; my brothers, Kasan Goh, Kajin Goh, and Kakim Goh; my sister-in-law, Camilla Prizeman; my nephews, Kio Kee Goh and Johnny Goh; my niece, Xian Goh; and my in-laws, Margaretha Hogeling, Anton Hogeling, Marcia Hogeling, Kevin David King, and Yaron Golombick.

I'd also like to thank Lydia Nagai for my author's headshot. I am thankful to Susanna Uchatius, Joanne Arnott, and Lenore Rowntree for their endorsements.

I owe my heartfelt gratitude to the support and inspiration of my incredible artistic community: Yun-Jou Chang, Alex Bruhanski, Scott Swan, Minah Lee, Sarah Wang, Jivesh Parasram, Julia Siedlanowska, Paula LaBrie, Alfonso Chin, Oscar Vargas, Candelario Andrade, Jay Hirabayashi, Jean-Francois Boisvenue, Malcolm Noel Dow, Mary Jane Paquette, Jessica Mary Keenan, Janice Jacinto, Ana Smith, Angelo Moroni, Rena Del Pieve Gobbi, Maria Salomé Nieto, Fraser Mackenzie, Jim Wong-Chu, Joy Kogawa, Tom Sandborn, Mary Ellen Copeland, Jon Kabat-Zinn, Geoff McMurchy, Yuri Arias, Kait Blake, Galen Yeo, Angeline Swee, Salman Husein, Imtiaz Popat, Joe Fitzpatrick, Kirk Moses, Ron Korb, Gretchen Jordan-Bastow, Summer Pervez Sultan, Steven Webb, Jay Hamburger, Christine Hayvice, Rena Graham, Mark den Boer, Heather Sangster, Robyn Hall, Veronique West, Emily Olsen, Ying Wang, Nancy Keough, Cindy Lou Griffith, Marni Norwich, Marlow Gunterman, Venus Soberanes, Jeremy Kyle, Keiko Honda, Haley Cameron, Noriko Nasu-Tidball, Angela Krewenchuk, Seth-Adrian Harris, Jabbar Al Janabi, Anton Côté Iorga, David Granirer, Sarah Jickling, Victoria Maxwell, Bernadine Fox, Sean Muldoon, Jenna-ka Clow, Ivan E. Coyote, Elizabeth Ruth, Jodi Lundgren, Shaena Lambert, Timothy Taylor, Cathleen With, Betsy Warland, Wayde Compton, Andrew Chesham, Leanna Brodie, Kathleen Flaherty, Jamie Reid, Bud Osborn, Carmen Aguirre, Jan Derbyshire, Tetsuro Shigematsu, C.R. Avery the man of musical bravery, Laurie Bricker, Bryn Genelle Ditmars, Tanya Evanson, Susan Katz, Sharon Taylor, Katheryn Petersen a.k.a. Salmon Avalanche, Shane Koyczan, S.R. Duncan, Rodney DeCroo, Rupix Kube, Angus Adair a.k.a. "The Svelte" Ms. Spelt, David Gowman a.k.a. Mr. Fire-Man, Rainy, Gabriel Martin, Joel Snowden, Kedrick James, Jen Lam, Al Mader, the Minimalist Jug Band, D-Noh and Deadman, Sue Cormier, Maia Love, Kali Jones, Barbara Adler, Randy Jacobs a.k.a. RC Weslowski, Vincy Kamberk, Fernando Raguero, Ruth Kozak, Candice James, Diane Laloge, Naomi Narvey, Neil Aitken, Fiona Tinwei Lam, Evelyn Lau, Andrea Thompson, Rachel Flood, Marcello Bruno, Rae Weinfeld a.k.a. Radar, Kyprios, Emily Lamb a.k.a. Magpie Ulysses, Bonnie Nish, Sita Carboni, Daniela Elza, Trina Ferguson,

Joël Tibbits, Jacques Lalonde, MarFer Douglas, Warren Dean Fulton, Kyle Hawke, Elly Litvak, Ron Carten, Glen Pavlick, Patrick Michael, Sarah Toolan, Bob Krzyzewski, Dave Macintosh, Rose Ananda Heart, Siobhan McCarthy, George Csaba Koller, Renee Rodin,Wanda Kehewin, Seia Roots, Ariadne Sawyer, Irwin Oostindie, Karen Ngan, Peggy Ngan,Vinetta Lenavat, Lisa Moore, Beverly Walker, Sean Tang, Ken Wan, and the loving memory of T. Paul Ste. Marie, Mary Seki, Harry Jones, Akihide John Otsuji, Billy Little, Gerry Gilbert, David Morgan, Jill Ineson, Irene Livingston, Roger Howie, Nicholas Epperson, Alex Winstanley, and Vladimir Vostok a.k.a. Zee Chillah (we miss you guys).

Salutations to the Kettle Friendship Society, Cinevolution Media Arts Society, Theatre Terrific, Rumble Theatre, Bruhanski Acting Studio, Seacoast Studios, Simon Fraser University's the Writer's Studio, Humber School for Writers, Historic Joy Kogawa House, Playwrights Theatre Centre, KW Studios, Baghdad Café, Pamela Bentley's Chicken Sessions, the Church of Pointless Hysteria, Bukowski's, Café Montmartre, Black Sheep Books, Octopus East, People's Co-op Bookstore, the Vancouver Poetry Slam at Café Deux Soleils, the Scribblers critiquing group, Pandora's Collective, Metro Living Zine, Yactac Gallery, W2 Media Café, Rhizome Café, the Connection Project, and Vancouver Co-op Radio's *Wax Poetic*, *World Poetry Café*, *Both Sides Now*, and *Radio Free Rainforest*.

Mad Love
and
Love Madly.

Yours humbly,
God's Glorified Secretary

About the Author

PHOTO BY LYDIA NAGAI

Kagan Goh was born in Singapore in 1969. After years of travelling, he immigrated with his family to Canada in 1986 and now resides in Vancouver. He is a spoken word poet, playwright, actor, mental health advocate and activist.

Kagan has been published in several anthologies, including *Strike the Wok: An Anthology of Contemporary Chinese Canadian Fiction* (TSAR Publications), *Henry Chow and Other Stories from the Asian Canadian Writer's Workshop* (Tradewinds Books), *Solamente en San Miguel: A Literary Celebration, Volume III* (San Miguel Literary Sala) and *Alive at the Center* (Ooligan Press). He has also been published in periodicals and magazines such as *Ricepaper*, *Misfit Lit*, *SARE: Southeast Asian Review of English*, and *Open Minds Quarterly*. In 2012, Select Books of Singapore published his debut book, *Who Let in the Sky?*

Goh is also an award-winning documentary filmmaker with a number of releases, including *Mind Fuck* (1996) and *Stolen Memories* (2012). His films have been broadcast on national television and screened at respected film festivals across Canada.

Surviving Samsara was also a multimedia multidisciplinary live theatrical production of the same name that incorporated dramatic performances, spoken word, music, and audiovisuals.